What Others Are Saying about James Robilotta and

LEADING IMPERFECTLY

"Each of us operates from a set of core values that directs how we work with others on a daily basis. James' book challenges us to hold true to our values and, at the same time, learn how to stretch and examine our vulnerabilities. This book provides great insight for everyone to consider."

— **Pat Leonard, Vice Chancellor for Student Affairs, University of North Carolina, Wilmington**

"I love the way James writes and speaks. His humor and storytelling make me laugh and touch my heart. I encourage you to read this book and become an authentic leader who transforms the hearts and minds of your team members."

— **Jon Gordon, Best-Selling Author of *The Energy Bus* and *The Carpenter***

"James is a hilarious guy who has a passion for developing authentic leaders, and this book proves both of those things."

— **Zhubin Parang, Writer, *The Daily Show with Jon Stewart***

"James' style is a great blend of humor and storytelling. He really keeps the reader engaged from beginning to end while sneaking in valuable lessons along the way. This is an important book to read because all leaders—even the very best—are leading imperfectly."

"James uses the perfect combination of hilariously true stories and very impactful lessons throughout his book. His message is the perfect model for young leaders and professionals, and not a single reader will be left uninspired! I truly cannot recommend this book enough!"

"This book will have you laughing out loud in one moment and deep in introspective thought the next. James' powerful message—it's more than okay to be imperfect as a leader—is one that needs to be heard by entry level professionals all the way up to C-level executives."

"James' ideas and style are perfect for any current or aspiring leader. Hitting on themes like vulnerability, authenticity, failure, and humanity, he looks at leadership in a different way, but in a way we probably should have been looking at it all along. This book is the perfect field manual, whether you're leading a team, a family, a company, or any other organization that wants to inspire, motivate, and encourage."

"I am the CEO of a company and have led numerous companies and people in my career. I have also been led. Upon reading James's book, I found much to take away, but most importantly as a leader, and more importantly as a person, the most dead-on advice that determines success as a leader and in life is 'Be who you are.' If you can be who you are to yourself and those you touch, then success as a leader and in life will follow."

— **Michael J. Smolenski, President and CEO of Coil-Tainer, LTD.**

"This is one of those books that makes you forget you're even reading. James' writing style is so conversational and unique that you feel like you're having a conversation with him. His points about leadership aren't ones you'll hear in a classroom or anywhere else. This book really makes you reflect on how and why you're leading."

— **Jess Ekstrom, Founder and CEO of Headbands of Hope**

"Readers will be inspired and motivated by this unique, humorous, and intelligent perspective on how to tap into your authenticity. James is one of the most authentic students ever to grace my college classroom, and he now provides others with a fresh approach to leadership in his first book. Although optional, expect to smile ear-to-ear or laugh out loud while reading!"

— **Joanne E. Nottingham, Ph.D., Leadership Studies Program Coordinator, University of North Carolina, Wilmington, and Leadership Coach**

"As the president of a university, I found James' book to validate what is important in leadership—begin with the imperfect and fill in the needed skills and strengths from others. His book is one I will encourage my staff to read because it is so important to be authentic and relatable when supporting and challenging our students."

— Dr. Sue Henderson, President of New Jersey City University

"James offers a riveting and thoughtful perspective on life and leadership. His engaging sense of reality will pull you in as you read through each inspiring chapter."

— Rick Daniels, Director of Student Life at Rock Valley College, and Author of *Tap Dancing Without Shoes: The History of Stepping and the Impact on Greek Life and Popular Culture*

"Entertaining! Funny! Thought-provoking! This book is not your typical leadership type book because it offers a new way to examine leadership; it's a book designed to think about leadership differently. James provides a new perspective on leadership, challenging readers to think about what it means to be vulnerable leaders who seek authenticity. This book is a great resource for student affairs and higher education professionals at all levels and functional areas and for students seeking to learn about leadership. James proposes that by challenging us to lead from our faults and what we have learned from them, we become more effective leaders. This approach allows others to see us as more approachable, honest, and vulnerable. As a faculty member in a student affairs and higher education program, I know this book will stimulate discussion among students as they develop their own sense and definitions of leadership. I cannot wait to use it in class."

— Tony W. Cawthon, Alumni Distinguished Professor of Student Affairs and Higher Education at Clemson University

"I recently had the opportunity to see James speak about his thoughts on authentic leadership. The way he delivered his message made him both relatable and respectable. This book reads just the way James speaks, and that is a great thing."

— **Peter van Stralen, CEO, Sunshine Brands, and Author of *C.A.R.E. Leadership***

LEADING IMPERFECTLY

The value of being authentic for leaders, professionals, and human beings

JAMES T. ROBILOTTA

AVIVA
PUBLISHING

Published by:
Aviva Publishing
Lake Placid, NY
518-523-1320
www.AvivaPubs.com

James Robilotta
Email: JamesTRobo@gmail.com
www.JamesTRobo.com

ISBN: 978-1-943164-11-0
Library of Congress: 2015905833

Editor: Tyler Tichelaar
Cover Designer: Diana Kolsky – DianaKolsky.com
Logo Designer: Allison Cleveland
Interior Book Layout: Fusion Creative Works – Fusioncw.com
Author Photo: Brian Furbush – BrianFurbush.com

Every attempt has been made to source properly all quotes.

Printed in the United States of America
First Edition
2 4 6 8 10 12

To my awesome wife, Jacqueline, who put up with countless conversations about how I thought no one was going to read this book. Thank you for always letting me get that off my chest and then abruptly telling me I was wrong. Thank you for being my sounding board, my first editor, my contrarian, my motivator, and for reminding me that *my* story is good enough so I should write this book. I love you.

To my parents, John and Suzanne Robilotta: I know you always wanted me to read more as a child and to stop bugging you to play board games with me. But I am glad I chose to live life rather than read about it. Thank you for never holding me back and letting me fly. Making you proud has been a lifelong goal of mine because I love and look up to both of you. You are amazing role models and parents. My only hope is that you believe that as much as I know it.

My gratitude for their help or support in writing this book goes to Chris Bruno, Sam Davidson, Justin Jones-Fosu, Antonio Neves, Patrick Snow, Jon Gordon, Jessica Ekstrom, Michael Smolenski, Jacqueline Robilotta, John J. Robilotta, Jr., Suzanne Robilotta, John P. Robilotta, and Brian Robilotta. Also, thank you to Brookton's Market in Brooktondale, New York, where I did most of my writing listening to Ben Howard, drinking tea and eating grilled cheese sandwiches.

CONTENTS

PREFACE
A NOTE TO THE READER

"I just finished my first book, I think I'll read another."
— Rodney Dangerfield

Welcome to my first attempt at writing a book. If you're reading this and you're not a family member, that probably means things are going better for me than expected! Before we dive in, here are some delightful facts I think you should know about me:

I think chocolate and peanut butter is the greatest combination of any two things ever. I can't stand when guys tie their ties too short; please get it to your belt buckle. I have a number of random food quirks: for example, I eat all of my potatoes before eating my steak or cheeseburger because I can't stand cold potatoes. I think paying for a cold sandwich is weird; the least you can do is melt the cheese. Also, I absolutely love applesauce. I grew up in Sayville, New York— voted friendliest town in America in 1994. Poorly timed stoplights infuriate me—why would they turn red if there is no one coming from that direction?

Randomly, for some time while living in New York City, I paid my rent by freestyle rapping. In 2009, I created an improv team that incorporates freestyle rapping and beatboxing into long-form improv. That team, North Coast, has since been featured on MTV and in publications such as *The New York Times, TimeOut New York* and *The Village Voice*, and it has headlined comedy festivals around North America.

Potentially more pertinently, I have been working in various leadership development capacities since 2001, predominantly in the higher education sector. I am now a full-time professional speaker and a personal coach who speaks to willing and unwilling corporate and college audiences internationally. All right, that's enough credentialing; let's chat about why I am writing this book:

Let me take you back to Mrs. Pumpernickel. Remember her? She was your first grade teacher. Do you recall that one time you were in the grocery store with your parents when you were six years old? Mrs. Pumpernickel was in there, looking at cantaloupes, wearing jeans, and pushing some baby around in her cart. You went up to her and asked her what she was doing outside of the school. Up until that day, you had assumed she lived in the school. She slept in a Murphy bed in the back of the classroom and ate rectangle pizza every day. She said she was picking up a few things for her family and that the baby was her son. You were flabbergasted! Mrs. Pumpernickel surely never ventured beyond her classroom or the cafeteria.

The next day you went to school, sat at your desk, looked at Mrs. Pumpernickel, and realized she was so much more than just your teacher. She was a mommy and someone's significant other; she didn't always wear a dress, and, apparently, she enjoyed cantaloupe from time to time! You looked at her differently after that, in a good way.

That's why I opened this book with a list of some of my idiosyncrasies. (Feel free to reach out to my wife for the unabridged version.) Sure, I wrote this book and, yes, people consider me a leader, but before we get into all that, I wanted you to know that I am a fellow human being. Do you have any fun food quirks? How about pet peeves or unique habits? We all do. Let's find something we have in common and then grow our relationship from there.

I see a problem in today's developing leaders—they think they need to be someone they are not to get what they want. This mentality negatively impacts the way they communicate and build relationships with their peers, coworkers, and supervisors.

Imagine if, instead of trying to spend so much energy trying to be someone you are not, you allow yourself to be human—to be you. It is for this reason I propose that leadership should stem from remembering we are human and leading from our faults. It is my firm belief that leaders of organizations and teams must first be seen as relatable and approachable if they want to ensure long-term loyalty and success. Doing so increases open and honest communication between all levels of the hierarchy because you will then be leading from a place of support and understanding instead of one of fear and pressure.

I also feel the best thing we can do for those who follow us is to be vulnerable and developmental through our own stories. With that in mind, welcome to my writing style: delightfully witty, occasionally punny, and full of deeply introspective personal storytelling. The mood I've tried to create in these pages is "old friends having a conversation at 11 p.m. at a late-night, greasy eatery." I don't know what genre that is; I didn't do well in high school English.

LEADING IMPERFECTLY

If you have ADHD like me, then feel free to read this book's chapters in any order. Each one has its own stand-alone message. I do not have the concentration to write a book this long with a huge story arch. So go ahead: read the introduction; then flip to the Contents page and see what strikes your fancy. For my "Type A" friends, the book still works if you want to read it straight through.

It is my humble opinion that we, as humans, can only learn things from people who are imperfect. We cannot learn things from people who are perfect. So thank you for coming on this thoughtful journey with me. I look forward to being imperfect with you.

INTRODUCTION

What Version of Yourself Do You Allow Others to See?

Do you get in where you fit in, or fit in where you get in, or neither? Who are you? Who knows you, like actually knows you? What version of yourself do you allow others to see? If I were going to ask your partner, your flight attendant, your parents, your grocery bagger, your coworker, and your best friend to tell me about you, would any of their answers overlap? Are you kind? Do you ask questions and care about the responses? If you showed people more of you, would they respect you more or question your relationship? Who would benefit from knowing you better? Who would benefit from knowing your story? Are you an authentic leader?

I have been there, friends. Heck, I am there. I am imperfect, and I struggle with who gets to know that about me. When I was at my senior prom, I dislocated my right knee dancing to Shania Twain's unfortunate hit, "Man, I Feel Like a Woman." I was put on probation as a student leader because my grades were mediocre at best. I have no idea how to do my taxes, and I am terrible at wrapping presents. I should have been fired from my last job because of how terrible I am with paperwork. The more I share my imperfections, however, the more connections I make, the more people relate to my story, the more people say they look up to me, and the better leader I become.

The answers to the questions above and many more are what I know you will get out of this book. You will learn the price of trying to come off as perfect in your organization. Understand the role that love must play in leadership. Recognize what it means to own the true you. Become conscious of how your morals must play a role in your decision-making process as a leader. Appreciate the difference between being a role model and being a hero. Grasp how to be a better public speaker by being more real to your audiences. Most importantly, you will come to realize that *your story is good enough*.

So why am I writing this book? That's a question I ask myself a lot. I also ask myself, "Who am *I* to write a book?" Writing this book has been one of the most polarizing adventures I have put my self-esteem through. At the end of the day, I wrote this book because my story is good enough. Sure, I have advised and supervised hundreds of people, I have spoken to tens of thousands internationally, and I am both a personal and leadership coach, but at the end of the day, I am still me. I am still curious. I am still learning. I am still imperfect. This book was an opportunity for me to share my story and tell you why I think authenticity is the most important facet of leadership.

This book is for student leaders, professionals, and human beings. It is for people in sales where authenticity leads to longer-term clients. It's for student affairs professionals and the student leaders they work with. It is for C-Level executives who will either be validated for already being authentic leaders or who will be woken up to the power of being imperfect. This book is for you, fellow human. Let this book serve as a guide to you becoming more self-aware as a leader. Let this journey open your eyes more to those around you, both in and out of the workplace. Taking the time to understand yourself and others will allow you to build rapport more quickly, create true loyalty, make more connections, and sell more, all the while feeling better about yourself. Be imperfect with me. Let's get started....

CHAPTER I
WHAT IS YOUR STORY?

Your Story Is Good Enough.

I was once asked in an interview, "What advice would you give to educators who want to inspire students?" In short, my answer was: Stop telling other people's stories and start telling your own.

This advice applies to everyone, not just educators working with students. In reality, whether we choose to admit it or not, we are all educators. We all, at some point in time, have the opportunity to teach and inspire someone else. Though I often see through the lens of an educator-student relationship, these principles still apply to many other types of relationships, including supervisor-supervisee, parent-child, sibling-sibling, and peer-peer.

As a professional speaker, one of the perks of my career is that I get to hear a lot of other speakers. For my own personal and professional development, I frequently watch a lot of commencement speeches, slam poetry, and TED talks online. I also attend up to ten conferences a year where I listen to my colleagues do their thing.

LEADING IMPERFECTLY

One of my *biggest* pet peeves is when I hear a speaker quote Gandhi, Martin Luther King, Jr., Mother Teresa, Nelson Mandela, etc. Quoting one of the greats is easy, hack, and clichéd. Everyone does it, so everyone's heard it before. Lately, I have also seen a number of speakers using overplayed YouTube clips in their presentations. While these videos are sometimes inspirational, they are almost always clichéd. We are better than this!

If I wanted to hear someone else's story, I would talk to that person, watch her video, or read her biography. If I'm listening to you, I want to hear your story. Quoting the same individuals and watching the videos everyone has already seen doesn't share anything new. Certainly for me, it is not the best use of my words because I am none of those people, and nor will I ever be. If I hear one more time that Michael Jordan got cut from his high school basketball team or that Wayne Gretzky said, "You miss 100 percent of the shots you don't take," I may boil over. Shout out to Susan B. Anthony, Steve Jobs, Ralph Waldo Emerson, and Eleanor Roosevelt. Everyone whom I have listed and many whom I haven't are amazing. They are heroes, societal game changers, the best at what they did, the most innovative, stupendously impressive, and worthy of all of the respect and admiration we can offer.

But here is what we have to remember, mentors:

Today's students will become us before they become the world's future heroes.

Attempting to inspire a student, mentee, peer, family member, etc., by suggesting he or she be more like one of the individuals above makes as much sense as trying to motivate a small boy who wants to be a lumberjack with Paul Bunyan's story. It's an amazing tale, but it's unrealistic. Instead, introduce that boy to the local logger who is climbing the ladder of success.

My suggestion is not to limit our mentees and our audiences from dreaming big. My suggestion is either to pair or replace the idealized stories with our own. I am saying that we need to give those who look up to us realistic, palpable examples and steps for how to chase down those dreams.

Quotes are an efficient and effective way to springboard into a point, but speakers, educators, and advice-givers who quote these great leaders and then drop the mic are doing it wrong. It is only after we break down quotes and follow them up with examples relevant to our audience that we can lead and inspire others.

We have a better shot at inspiring others by sharing our own stories—where we succeeded, where we slipped, and what we learned from both. Inspiring students with personal and tangible examples of things like: creating change, following passion, being better leaders, making a difference, and/or being more socially and globally conscious will expose them to more substantial true-to-life approaches to how to do the hardest thing: start.

Ready for the good news, my fellow educators, supervisors, parents, big siblings, and best friends?

Your story is good enough.

Sometimes. we feel the need to tell others' stories because we are self-conscious about our own not having enough merit. We think,

"What have I done?" and "Who wants to hear about my boring life?" I know this feeling well. Believe me; that is the exact reason I spoke for free for a lot of years. Who wanted to hear my story, let alone pay for it?

I started presenting my ideas at conferences as a student leader in 2001. In 2007, I was booked for my first speech at a school other than my own. In 2009, I got paid for the first time as a keynote speaker. Even after that, I still spoke for free most of the time until I joined a speaking agency in 2011.

After 2007, I started considering speaking as a career more seriously because a conference attendee came up to me after one of my sessions and asked a simple question, "How much do you charge?" Until then, I just loved sharing ideas and being in front of people—I hadn't considered that I would have a story people would want to listen to, much less pay me to hear. Even after that, as much as I wanted to be a speaker, I still wasn't convinced.

I figured that since I hadn't loss a limb in a war, or been involved in some intense alcohol or drug misuse, or been a victim of any kind, no one would pay to hear my story. Heck, I didn't have a story; I was a nobody. Beyond that, I thought no one *should* pay me because I was a privileged white boy who grew up in the friendliest town in America, had his college tuition paid by his parents, and was free from any traumatic experiences.

Well, that's not exactly true. There was the time in first grade when the most beautiful girl I had ever laid my six-year-old eyes on, Kate, was laughing on the other side of the playground. The school bully saw me looking at her and challenged me to a race. He said the first one over to her could hold her hand. We didn't think to ask Kate her opinion on this. So we took off running. Tragically, right before I got to her, I either fell or the bully tripped me. For the sake of a better story that makes me into more of a sympathy-earning protagonist, let's say he tripped me. I fell to the concrete and used my perfectly-fine, pre-fall left arm to try to slow down my descent. Alas, I broke my once-perfectly-fine, pre-fall left arm. My first grade teacher didn't believe me when I said it was broken; instead, she yelled at me to stop crying on our way through the school to the nurse. Even in this story, it kind of worked out: I got a small win when I walked in the next day with a cast and my teacher's jaw hit the floor. Bigger win: having a cast in first grade was actually kind of cool, and best of all, Kate signed it.

Really, other than a broken arm in first grade, nothing traumatic or crazy-life-altering happened to me, so I told myself I did not have a story worth listening to.

Then people started coming up to me after my talks to tell me how they really related to what I was saying, and they shared similar experiences. They told me they could see themselves in my stories about my self-esteem struggles, supervisors and supervisees I have worked with, and my failed and successful attempts holding peers accountable who were not being authentic. They really appreciated how relatable I was. They also loved how I used humor to hit my points and keep them engaged. Turns out, I had a story all along; I just needed to trust it and be authentic in telling it.

I have won awards and received tons of support from my wife and family, who I know are proud of me. I have received so many speaking requests that I became a fulltime speaker and personal coach in August of 2013. The feedback I get from my presentations is 98 percent super-positive. But our self-esteem is a persistent beast, my friends. To this day, I still find it unsettling that companies and universities spend the money they do to bring me in. I do not always think I deserve the accolades I have graciously been given, but I am proud that I earned them on the back of my own stories.

I am here to stress that your story is plenty powerful. If mine is, I promise yours is, too. Your story is light-years more accessible to others than Maya Angelou, Stephen Hawking, Helen Keller, or William Shakespeare's; therefore, it is much more effective in inspiring others than you trying to tell someone else's. You have experienced something in your life that, if told at the right place and time, could really make an impact on someone. Take time to reflect on your past and find your story.

What have you been through? When was a time that you felt proud of yourself? Have you done anything random? Have you had any spontaneous deep talks with someone you did not expect to have one with? What's the hardest conversation you've ever had? How do you specifically live out your definition of happiness? We all have stories, and if you're having trouble thinking of one, then it's time to take some more risks and create some!

Personally, I like to live in such a manner that I'll always be generating new stories. That means if I have the opportunity to do something extremely random, I will jump on it just so I can talk about it afterwards. I find myself in these situations by always saying, "Yes" to the story. One of my favorite professors in college, Dr. Dragna, once said, "The moment is more important than what comes after the moment." I consider that to be one of my life's mottos.

WHAT IS YOUR STORY?

By saying, "Yes" in the moment, I've had some of the most fascinating conversations. There was the 4 a.m. Waffle House talk with a local female stripper and a male sex worker in Wilmington, North Carolina. I chatted with a full-time oyster shucker in Baton Rouge, and I shared a plane convoy with the head of the Arizona Farmers' Bureau. I randomly shot the breeze with Zack Galifianakis about rural North Carolina. One time, I was even flown to Detroit to be in a TV pilot as a host of a new game show—all because of a conversation I had with some seemingly random guy after a show I was in.

As authentic leaders, we must have the courage to find our story and share it with others. Share the times you have fallen short, hurt others, let yourself down and what you did to bounce back and regain control. Share the times you triumphed, made yourself and others proud, did something you did not know you were capable of, and how it felt. Stop telling Mark Zuckerberg, Henry Ford, Oprah Winfrey, and John F. Kennedy's stories because most people can't relate to them; we can only relate to your telling of your story.

Sure, I have a dream that we will challenge and support each other to shoot for the moon, to be the change we wish to see, and to dance like no one is watching. But I'm going to do it with my story because it's good enough, and it is the best one I know how to tell. How about you? What's your story, and who needs to hear it?

CHAPTER 2
DO YOU LEAD FROM YOUR FAULTS?

You're the only one who has to fall asleep to the sound of your heartbeat.

I will admit it—I want people to like me. Okay, I'll be even more honest—I *need* people to like me. For much of my life, I have based my happiness on how others react to me. Letting my self-esteem rest in others' opinions has not exactly been my healthiest life choice.

For example, when I was in college at University of North Carolina-Wilmington, I had a buddy, Stephen. Stephen was one of the best-dressed people I ever met. I admired the way people would compliment him, and I would even let his opinions on what I wore dictate my mood that day. I started to change the way I dressed and bought new clothes and shoes that I really had no business buying as a broke college student. But, in my mind, when he would tell me I was looking "fresh," it was worth it; I would strut around campus, winking and pointing at anyone who looked my way. Well, not really, because that would have been creepy, but I did carry myself with more confidence because Stephen thought my outfit was on point.

To this day, I continue to center different aspects of my life on others' opinions. I frequently forgo my own plans just to be there for someone else because I fear that person will think ill of me if I don't show up for her. This past week, I committed to writing more. To support my goal, on Wednesday I blocked off a ton of time to get down to business. I went to a local sandwich spot, got a bite to eat, and started typing away for approximately forty-two minutes. Then my new friend, Darnell, hit me up and asked whether I wanted to grab lunch. Now, not only did I have grandiose plans of writing all day, but I had also just eaten. So what did I do? I reactively said, "Sure! I can meet up with you!" and drove across town to meet him at a different sandwich spot closer to where he was.

I can keep going; I have examples for days. Currently, I'm on a plane from Indianapolis to D.C. and it's before sunrise. The guy across the aisle from me is really enjoying looking at the lit up cities we are flying over and the gorgeous stars we can see high above the light pollution. So, instead of pulling out my laptop, which would inevitably cause glare on his window and taint his view, I pulled out my phone, dimmed the brightness all the way down, and am now writing these words in my notes to email to myself later. This man does not know me, and he certainly does not know that I've racked my brain over "the right thing to do" in this situation for the past ten minutes.

I am not sharing these stories because I want a gold star. I am sharing these examples because my accommodating logic is astoundingly preposterous at times. In the case of the airplane fellow, we do not know one another, we probably will never see each other again, we both paid the same amount for our seats, and, within reason, we are both entitled to whatever activity helps us pass the time! Why do I care so much about what he thinks of me?

These are just three examples of *many*. One of the positive ways I have spun my need for others to like me is by being a true social chameleon. I have the innate ability to fit in to whatever group I interact with because I ask questions until I find the thing people are passionate about…all because I want to feel accepted. I sometimes even unconsciously change the way I speak based on the region I am in or the type of people I am around. I am the conversational equivalent of being a "jack of all trades, master of none."

What would you like to talk about? Hip-hop? Fashion? Need a restaurant recommendation? Gender equality? LGBT issues? Relationships? Marine life? The meaning of life? Golf? Cars? Comedy? Leadership? Sailing? Social media? Religion? Traveling? Applesauce? You get my point.

Here is my struggle, though: Because I share different aspects of myself to relate with or accommodate people, does that mean I am being fake? Never in a conversation do I claim to know everything about what we're talking about. In fact, when a conversation goes a little deeper into a topic that I don't know much about, I rarely hesitate to say something like, "Yeah, I'm not proud about this, but I don't really follow politics that closely, so I don't have an opinion on the deficit," or "I've heard of that band, but I couldn't tell you anything they sing." I don't pretend to know things I don't, but I imagine others leave conversations with me thinking I am equally passionate about dove-tail joints, finding purpose in life, or loom-weaving technology. I do have a genuine desire to engage with my conversation mate, so if I try to appear more knowledgeable about a topic just so you think

I'm "good people" and want to keep talking to me, is that wrong? Part of me is proud of this chameleon-type talent, but the other part fears being called inauthentic; in fact, that is one of my biggest fears.

I think we all can name a time when we behaved inauthentically because we thought we would gain something in that moment. Maybe it was to look cooler, feel smarter, suck up to a potential connection, get the promotion, or just prove a point. If you don't think you have ever done this, consider your past job interviews. Job interviews are the one setting where inauthentic behavior is practically expected.

A popular piece of advice for interviewees who are asked the question: "What is a weakness you have?" is *Answer with a weakness that is really a strength.*" Say things like, "I'm too reliable and am often asked to help on additional projects. My weakness is that I don't know how to say, 'No,'" or "I'm a perfectionist and a workaholic—everything I take on has to be done quickly and well," or "I am hyper-organized—like, I color-coordinate my underwear when I'm putting away my laundry." Well, maybe you wouldn't share your underwear habits with your future employer, but you get my point. What if instead of giving fake, non-answers to interview questions like this one, we all collectively agreed to be vulnerable and share our authentic selves. Employers could have the benefit of an honest snapshot of a potential employee to determine accurately her growth potential. Interviewees could feel more relaxed and genuine in interview settings instead of delivering canned answers. Alas, my adorable book is not going to change the way interviews are conducted across the world so give me just a second to come down off my soapbox and hop onto another one.

DO YOU LEAD FROM YOUR FAULTS?

The phrase "Fake it till you make it," is thrown around a lot when it comes to chasing your dreams, applying for jobs, and just trying to win at life. The idea that we should all fake having a certain skill set or status in order to wiggle our way into the circles or scenarios we want to be part of is misguided. I agree with the sentiment to a certain extent, but I believe an important follow-up to this phrase should be:

> "Fake it till you make it, but if all you ever do is fake it, you'll never really make it."

"Fake it till you make it" only makes sense for a little while. What we are faking in most cases is self-confidence, and it is easy to see the value in having confidence in oneself. Many times, we have the skills and talents required to get to where we need to go, but we get in our own way and convince ourselves we cannot achieve what we want. So, by portraying ourselves as someone we don't think we are, we are essentially taking the side-door into the self-confidence party. It would take too long to wait out front in the line of excuses and self-doubt while trying to get in the front door.

Therefore, if we need to fake it for a little to help us get in the building and trick our low self-esteem, let's give ourselves that pass. The larger issue is when people feign being something they are not for extended periods of time. How many movies has Hollywood cranked out that have "faking it" as the core message? Here's a few: *Aladdin*, *A Bronx Tale*, *Hitch*, *Mean Girls*, *Wedding Crashers*, *Mrs. Doubtfire*.... We are bombarded not only by popular stories of faking it, but we witness inauthenticity in our peers and coworkers as well—people who spend their time trying to be seen as perfect.

Leadership is a team effort, and it's not only about getting everyone to the goal. It's also about the learning, teaching, and growing that happens along the way. Individuals who are trying to be seen as perfect, in my eyes, are missing the point of leadership.

As humans, we can only learn things from people who are imperfect. We cannot learn things from people who are perfect.

One of the first people I remember exhibiting this lesson of imperfection in my life was my high school guidance counselor, Mr. Dillon. Mr. Dillon was the man. He was a super cool guy whom I loved spending time with. I would make up excuses to go to his office so I could just sit and talk with him about life.

Looking back at it, Mr. Dillon possessed many great attributes that made him someone I looked up to. First and foremost he was approachable. He had a welcoming spirit and was appreciative of the time you gave him. He was also funny. Mr. Dillon was not afraid to take a quick jab at you, which never felt out of place. Instead, it made you feel like you and he were closer. Conversations with him had a great balance between talking about academics and about life.

What I valued the most about Mr. Dillon was that I never felt he was talking down to me. Instead, he took the time to get to know me as a person. Our age gap did not matter, and I personally never even thought about it. When I would share things I was struggling with or choices I was juggling between, he was quick to insert a personal story about himself and a time he went through something similar.

Mr. Dillon made me feel like I was going to be okay despite not having it all figured out or knowing all of the answers. He was a realist. He was not afraid to call me out when I was slipping and celebrate with me when I succeeded. And when it came time to look at colleges, Mr. Dillon's advice was spot on because he took the time to get to know me, so he knew where I was competent and where I needed to be pushed. I trusted him because Mr. Dillon showed me that he was a fellow human being. I knew when he had slipped and when he had soared. Without realizing it at the time, Mr. Dillon was a leader to me because he knew how to lead by sharing his faults, which brings me to my proposition:

We must lead from our faults.

As leaders, it is not enough to have messed up and learned from it. While that is the first step, we rarely get to step two: sharing our story. Sharing your story is essential for two reasons: The first is obvious; we want others to learn from our mistakes so they don't make the same ones. On a very basic level, mistakes can be costly, so avoiding them can increase the efficiency of our operations. Imagine the potential time and money saved from collectively sharing and learning from mistakes. The next reason, however, is the crux of authentic leadership, and it has a huge impact on the long-term success of our organizations and the individuals within them.

The second reason we must lead from our faults is to allow others to see themselves in us. That is what Mr. Dillon did for me. When we are our authentic selves and reveal to others our humanity, we give them the opportunity to connect with us in the most dynamic way. Relatability is an extraordinarily powerful leadership tool because it naturally emphasizes connection. When I see a little of myself in the people above me, the idea of becoming as successful as that person becomes tangible. We gain confidence, we feel validated, and we are more eager to be active participants in creating success. Being more relatable also increases the likelihood of more honest communication; if we can see ourselves in someone, then we are more at ease. The more comfortable we are, the more likely we are to put ourselves out there and be more open during times of need and occasions when we seek advice or mentorship.

I remember learning the importance of making others comfortable while I was serving on a professional search committee during my undergrad years. A great friend and mentor of mine, Larry Wray, was the best interviewer I have ever seen. He exemplified a very simple but effective interviewing philosophy: the more comfortable everyone is, the better (read: more honest) the dialogue will be.

At the start of each interview, Larry would get up, greet the candidate with a huge smile and a warm handshake, and usually crack his first joke even before everyone sat down. Then, he would sit back in his chair and spend most of the rest of the interview in a relaxed position. Larry didn't have interviews; he had conversations. He would share with candidates that there were no set questions; he just wanted to get to know them. So he would share a little bit about our school, why it's an exciting and developmental place to work, intertwine everything with personal stories, and ask the interviewees for their feedback. He wanted to know what they did outside of work, what made them tick, and their philosophies on how best to develop leaders.

During the whole interview, I would watch the candidates, who at first would appear a little wary, slowly relax into the process. They would start to sit more casually, genuinely laugh, and allow themselves to get excited when the mood struck them. They shared personal opinions, not textbook interview answers. It was fun. The interview technique threw candidates off a little, but it also allowed their authentic personalities to shine through.

Candidates would leave the conversation feeling refreshed and excited because they were truly heard and allowed to be themselves.

> In minutes, Larry created an interviewing environment where people who had never met him before felt like they could talk to him for hours.

He had an amazing ability to make people feel more like they were out at the bar divulging life stories than at a huge job placement exchange.

Larry's secret is that he cared about fit first, skills second. He knew the kind of people who would mesh well with his current staff, help bring his vision for the organization to life, and also get the job done. If the candidate were hired, Larry also would be the person's supervisor, so he was trying to learn what this person would be like on a day-to-day basis. So in order to find the best candidate, he first had to be relatable with all of them and make them comfortable so they would bring their most authentic selves to the interviews.

Larry's genuine interest and curiosity would not stop after the interview. Those who were fortunate enough to be hired by Larry learned that open and real conversation with the goal of bringing out the best in his direct reports was also his supervision style. Larry created an environment where his employees could feel comfortable bringing up new ideas and feel confident that they would be heard. His leadership style established trust among his team and also allowed Larry's critical feedback to motivate people to be better instead of bitter.

Too often, we think that in order to lead those around us, we need to be the perfect example of what we want them to be. If you haven't realized it already, that could not be further from the truth. We put unneeded and unproductive pressure on ourselves to be perfect.

We must realize that we were selected for our positions not because we were the most perfect, but because we were the most trusted.

The most trusted to do the best job we can by using our strengths and motivating others to do the same. Fulfilling that trust means owning the things we are not great at and creating an environment where those around us can feel comfortable sharing in that practice. We must create a place where people feel confident sharing their struggles and asking for help. We must create a place where people trust that their requests for guidance are met with an open ear and thoughtful questions or ideas, not with a slap of "Just figure it out; I did, and so can you."

Being fake and feigning perfection is a lose-lose for both the organization and the individual. For the organization, open and honest dialogue will never occur. Employees will not feel comfortable asking for advice; therefore, they will be less effective and efficient.

DO YOU LEAD FROM YOUR FAULTS?

For the individual, being fake is a heavy burden; it's a lot of weight to carry around. Some of the perks might be nice in the short-term, like praise from a supervisor or positive attention from others. But, in the long run, fake people will live an isolated, guilt-filled life. Only you know whether you are being fake and how that feels; after all, you're the only one who has to fall asleep to the sound of your heartbeat. Instead, be honest with yourself and lead from your faults.

CHAPTER 3
WHAT IS ONE LIE YOU TELL YOURSELF?

You must own who you are before you can be real to others.

We must own who we are before we can be real to others. Simply put, we must "in-reach" before we "out-reach."

"In-reaching" is really about owning who you are. It's probably the hardest piece of authentic leadership. Heck, it's one of the hardest things in life! People are amazingly talented at judging other people. If you need proof, start reading YouTube comments on popular videos. We are champions at giving others both solicited and unsolicited advice. We are great at holding up a mirror for other people to look at themselves, and we are even better at making up excuses when we look at ourselves in that same mirror.

I am a firm believer that the best conversations we will have in our lives all occur after 10:00 p.m. at a diner, Waffle House, Steak 'n Shake, Perkins, IHOP, Denny's, or whatever your favorite late-night eatery is. There's something special about the later hours of the day that allows us to relax and open up. During these conversations, I like to ask deeper questions because I'm that guy in my friend circles. One of my favorite questions I will ask you now is:

What is one lie you tell yourself every single day?

Now, before you start thinking, I am not talking about when you say, "Oh, I'm going to go the gym today," or "I am going to catch up on all of the reading I need to do," or "I'll clean the bathroom." These may be little lies you tell yourself, but I'm thinking bigger. The lies above are not life-altering, invasive thoughts. Go deeper. *What is one lie you tell yourself every single day?*

I'll tell you about my lie. If you haven't skipped around chapters, you already know that since college, I have prided myself on the way I dress. A lot of people I meet tell me I am one of the best-dressed people they know. I pull off things others say they cannot because of "the confidence with which I carry myself." Those are very sweet things for people to tell me, but I always find the statement: "but you can pull it off," a little eyebrow-raising. That comment carries the same connotation to me as calling someone or something "interesting." Is "interesting" a compliment, or do you mean to say it's weird? Did you just shoot for the middle so as not to offend? When someone says, "But you can pull it off," I never know whether the person means "I admire you" or "I would never be caught dead in what you're wearing, but since I've already called attention to your outfit and am not sure how to tell you that, I guess I'll just say, 'But you can pull it off.'" While I don't always know how to take the comment, I try to appreciate the sentiments because I do try to dress well.

WHAT IS ONE LIE YOU TELL YOURSELF?

What people do not know is the reason why I dress well. I dress well because I have convinced my twisted brain that if I put a nice outfit over my body, people will pay attention to what I say and not how unattractive I am. My body embarrasses me, but I believe that by covering it, the people I interact with will just appreciate the freshness! (Insert uncomfortable laugh here.) In reality, I have developed an expensive coping mechanism for my self-consciousness regarding my weight. It is the most visible lie I tell myself every day. Have no fear, though; I have others!

Potentially, the bigger lie I have convinced people of is that I am very confident. I am a huge extrovert. I love being around people; it makes me feel energized and like I am on a high. I have loved being the center of attention since a very early age. There is a video of me when I was around age seven at my grandparents' fiftieth wedding anniversary banquet. At the dinner, everyone was sitting down and politely eating dinner except for me! I was up dancing to the extremely soft dinner music...and using the whole dance floor to do it. I was killing it. I'm sure there are even earlier examples of my love of attention, but you'll have to come over for a slideshow at Mama Robilotta's house for that.

Fast forward to today. When people ask me why I wanted to be a speaker, I offer two reasons: first, to make a life-changing impact on others through positivity and laughter, and second, because I love attention. The way I see it, it's a mutually beneficial relationship. A little for you, a little for me!

Here is the thing, though: Just because I am an extrovert and love being in front of people does not mean I am confident. As I've talked to fellow extroverts, I've found that it's actually a very common misconception about us. For me, a lot of my actual confidence stems from what others say about me—going back to my need to be liked.

I attribute most of my self-confidence issues to experiences in middle and high school. I was always the kid everyone knew and thought was super-funny. People wanted to sit next to me in class; they laughed at my tomfoolery, and they told me I was a good guy. But on weekends and after school, no one would want to hang out, and on Monday in class, I would find out everyone had been at a big party, but I did not even know it was going on! If I told you how girls treated me, you would think I was stealing Rodney Dangerfield's material so I will spare you from that. All you need to know is that they all thought I was a really great guy, but the friend-zone and I were very close friends.

My high school experience made me start thinking that when people said things to me, they didn't really mean them. I believed they were just placating me in the moment, but they really did not want to associate with me. This perception still impacts me heavily today. While each year I have taken back more and more control of my confidence, I still recognize the emphasis I put on others' opinions when I constantly ask for feedback and only rarely believe the positive compliments.

I come from a family where we each make passive-aggressive comments when we are trying to "look out for each other." To avoid the sting of a bitter comment, I learned to make fun of myself first.

Self-deprecating humor about my weight became a way of life for me. Most of my early stand-up comedy sets consisted of it as well. I would make fun of how fat I was left and right just to be the first to laugh at it. I used to say, "You can't tell when fat guys like me are wearing a belt, but you just appreciate the fact that it's hopefully there."

One day, after one of my earlier attempts at stand-up, I was talking to my buddy, Brian, who was in the audience during a set. I reflected on my performance and told him I got a few laughs here and there, but I concluded that my set needed to be tighter. Then, he told the truth. He said, "I think you got more groans than laughs." He went on to tell me the audience members were laughing because they were uncomfortable and felt bad for me, not because the jokes were particularly funny. He then twisted the dagger in one more time and told me that I behave the same way offstage all of the time, and it was depressing to be around; it was more sad than funny, and it often killed the vibe. Ouch.

I responded with something sassy like, "Well, that's just how I was raised, and I am sorry I am ruining your life!" But I knew inside that Brian was right, and no matter how hard it was for me to hear, I needed to own this feedback. I also knew he was speaking from a place of love, but that did not mean it did not hurt to hear. The truth was that my attempts to prevent people from making fun of my weight were just a defense mechanism. A defense mechanism that caused people to be uncomfortable around me, which, for a guy who has a deep desire for people to like him, was terrible and, more importantly, not who I was.

After I graduated from college and started my first job, it was interesting to see the way my attempts at confidence played out. I fluctuated between being almost cocky—defensive of my thoughts and actions—and questioning whether I was even good at my job. My supervisors during these years were pretty terrible at giving productive and timely feedback. One even made fun of me for asking to be evaluated. Everything I learned from them was reactive, never proactive. They showed no interest in being a part of my development on the front end where they could have asked questions that provoked thought, made me sharper, and more confident.

Since my supervisors largely left me alone, I developed my own leadership style. I called it "authentic leadership," thought it was brilliant, and just knew it would be a game changer in the leadership world. I then hopped online to buy the domain name and was promptly slapped in the face. I found out that not only was that domain taken, but more than that, Bill George had already written a book on the topic titled *Authentic Leadership*! I was deflated. Then, I began to feel validated—my philosophy and strategy of leadership was confirmed! For what it's worth, Bill George's book is wonderful and I definitely recommend it.

When I was a supervisor, one thing I always made sure to do with my staff members every year was let them know the professional development goals I was working on. Every August, I would sit down with my new team and have them set SMART (specific, measurable, attainable, relevant, and timely) goals. We would talk about our expectations of each other. I would also have them open up about what they each felt they could add to the team and in what areas the team would need to support them. I would share with my staff what I felt my added value was and in what ways I would need their assistance to hold me accountable.

I told them about how I was an exceptional listener, how I would push them both personally and professionally to be more open and present, and how I was on their team as a community builder.

WHAT IS ONE LIE YOU TELL YOURSELF?

I then let them know how I struggled with being a disorganized procrastinator. I got into my line of work to make an impact, not to do paperwork and answer emails all day. I cautioned them that sometimes they would send me an email, I would read it, and then I would promptly not respond. The email would then drift southward in my inbox throughout the day and potentially fall off the first page. If it did that, I told them, I had no idea where it went because I never looked beyond the first page.

I did not say that so later when they complained because my disorganization reared its ugly head, I could respond, "I warned you this is how it would be!" No, I told them about my weaknesses because I wanted them to hold me accountable—to help me get better—and I wanted to model owning and sharing my weaknesses. I knew I could not and should not hide areas I struggle in because I would be lying to myself and my team. Not to mention, my team would likely realize these things about me pretty quickly.

Very often, we are quick to say things like, "Well, that's just the way I am, so deal with it." That is *not* what owning who you are looks like. Such a statement is just super-lazy. It implies you have no desire to change or work on who you are.

The moment you think you have it all figured out is the exact moment you don't.

Instead, share who you are and ask others to *help you*, not "deal with you." In my case, I had no problem being confronted or called out by my staff. I think, when done at the appropriate time and place, development can and should go both ways.

49

Our first reaction to being called out is usually a defensive one. Whether we snap back at the person, make excuses, or jump into insincere apology mode, our reaction is understandable because our pride just got attacked. However, all feedback, when said respectfully, is worthy of reflection. We must begin the process of owning the lies we tell ourselves because only we know the weight that comes with lying to ourselves and how much it sucks to carry that weight around.

For me, writing this book has been a yin and yang between confidence and "What's the point?" On one hand, writing my opinions down has been quite self-affirming. If I am going to put my thoughts into the written word for mass-distribution, then I better believe in what I am saying! My speaking career has benefited from this process the most.

On the other hand, I worry whether anyone will like or respect what I write. I worry people will just blow through this book and not take my questions seriously. Will my readers just finish it and move on with their lives? Just today, I emailed a connection at a major publisher for this book. Receiving her response that she would love to connect has sent my brain into a tizzy. Questions I could have answered more confidently last week, now rack my headspace. Why is this book important? Who needs to hear my message, and why do they need to hear it from me? How do I make sure they not only hear it but follow up on it?

The past few years have been very affirming to me as a professional speaker. I was able to go out on my own in August of 2013 and grow my speaking and coaching business. I even started a life-coaching arm. I just got comfortable with owning my new career and answering the question, "What do you do?" with "I am an authentic leadership speaker and personal coach." But am I ready to call myself an author?

I own the fact that I have self-confidence issues. The process of working on them has been quite the pursuit. I know that I make more decisions for myself now than I ever have in the past, though. I no longer consult forty-seven different people every time something comes up in my life. The unwavering support of my wife and parents has also been critical in my drive to be proud of who I am.

How about you? Who is on your team? How have you grown, and where can you see marked improvements in your life from owning who you are? Have you started this process at work as well as at home?

Allow yourself to open up during times of excitement and fear to those around you. Appropriately timed honesty opens the door to deeper connections and more authentic interactions with people.

The time is now to start this process—to begin this journey, if you haven't already. You simply cannot be an authentic leader without first owning who you are, without "in-reaching." It is the most important facet of authentic leadership. Without doing this work, you cannot live your life on purpose to the fullest—you cannot be real to others. Talk it out with yourself, your partner, your counselor, your coach, etc. Take this time to own who you are.

CHAPTER 4
WHO GETS TO SEE YOUR IMPERFECTIONS?

We Are All Self-Conscious.

Kanye West claimed, in his song "All Falls Down," that he was the first person to admit being self-conscious. Though probably not the first person to admit to it, Mr. West certainly was one of the biggest hip-hop artists to do so. Sure, other rappers alluded to it before, but none of their tracks reached the same level of popularity as his song, which hit number seven on the Billboard charts in May of 2004. In a music genre traditionally filled with braggadocios boasting about why they are the best and the things they own that prove it, Kanye dropped some truth about what it was like coming up in a world before and during his fame. If you haven't heard "All Falls Down," give Kanye's track a listen to see what I mean.

"Hey, thanks for the hip-hop education, James; now what does Kanye West have to do with leadership?"

I'm glad you asked! Whether you choose to like Kanye West or not, in that moment, he was a role model for being real. In my experience, the most effective leaders are not afraid to be real with their followers. As a matter of fact, they strive to be genuine because they recognize the importance of the growth that occurs when being imperfect.

In a world run by social media, the concept of being real to one another has been stretched and manipulated. We can be whomever we want online. I have friends on Instagram who consistently post pictures of themselves next to cars that aren't theirs. Some of the people I follow on Twitter only post clichéd leadership quotes. And my Facebook friends, based on the pictures they post, eat only fancy foods.

The image most people project online is a streamlined head-in-the-clouds vision of how they define happiness, what they want their lives to look like, and what they care about. So if selectively choosing your social media posts is what you need to do to make you feel better, go ahead and do that. Fighting the battle of being your most authentic self by prioritizing your social media persona is backwards. We must look at our real-life persona first.

Allow me to re-ask then: What version of yourself do you allow others to see? If I were to ask your family, your supervisor, your supervisees, your best friends, the cashier at the supermarket, your ex, your last server, and others in your religious community all to tell me about you, would I get similar answers? Who would give me a different answer and why? One way to show you have been living a consistent, authentic life is if your friends from all areas of your life get along with each other. Their ability to do so shows that your values are congruent across your world.

Our speech patterns may fluctuate based on whom we are speaking to, but who you are at the core should not change. For example, we may not communicate with our supervisor that we are frustrated about a certain aspect of our job the same way we would vent about it to our buddies at the bar. If I felt like my supervisor was micro-managing me, I would request a meeting with him to talk about how I am frustrated, my desire for more autonomy, and how I can gain more of his trust. To my buddies, I would talk about how my boss will not get off my back and how I feel like a stifled puppet, but I am going to request a meeting with him to talk it over. I would use stronger words with my friends because they are a safer place, but the bottom line in both cases would be me discussing what I felt was right and standing up for myself to my supervisor. Remaining congruent at your core is a concept we frequently need to revisit. Unfortunately, it is hard to get others to think about this concept and see how their inconsistency impacts the bigger picture.

In my first job out of graduate school, I had a boss who truly believed she was never wrong and would go to preposterous lengths to prove her points to herself. Meanwhile, the rest of us saw right through her. Note that I am using the term "boss," not "supervisor" here; there is a difference between the two—a boss tells you what to do and is not developmental; a supervisor cares about your career potential and provides effective feedback and professional development. Let me tell you a story here so you'll understand how I developed my low opinion of this boss.

I was working as a resident director at a university in the Northeast. It was my job to oversee the first-year student population living on campus. One aspect of my job was to serve as a judicial hearing offi-cer for students who broke rules within our code of conduct. During this particular year, we had one student who was, quite frankly, a pain in the ass. He kept doing little things on the floors that would pick away at the community we were trying to form. For example, he would take people's whiteboard markers, rip down educational bulletin boards, and get drunk and draw penises on the hallway walls. Unfortunately, we could never catch him in the act so we could not effectively adjudicate him.

Then, one day, he thought it would be a good idea to steal some books from the bookstore. Apparently, he forgot the purpose of those tall sensors at the exit of every store. Alas for him, he was caught, so I set up a meeting with him to discuss the incident and decide about would-be consequences. My boss asked to sit in on his judicial hearing with me, which, when directly translated from my boss's language, actually meant: "I don't trust you so I am going to do it and you just sit there."

When the meeting date came a couple of days later, the three of us sat down in my office. She kicked off the meeting by asking him, over her ornate reading glasses, "So why did you do it?" Now, this gentleman had had a few days to think about this judicial hearing and the potential questions he might be asked. He'd had time to formulate a defense or reasonable explanation for his actions or maybe even come up with an apology. Instead, his response was a sassy, "Like you have never done anything wrong!" I concluded at that moment that this gentleman would never be a lawyer, or at least never my lawyer.

Though his response was childish at best, it was my boss' response that ruffled my beard. She took off her glasses, looked him dead in the eye, and said, straight-faced, "I haven't." In case you missed it, my boss just claimed, in front of a student, that she had *never* done anything wrong. I kept my mouth shut because I wanted to keep my job for a little while longer. The student did not keep his mouth shut. He decided to call her out on this obvious lie. He responded to her claim with examples of things she may have done wrong at some point just to make sure. "Right, so you've never rolled through a stop sign; you've never done two miles an hour over the speed limit; you've never jaywalked or sent a text while driving?" She looked him back, dead in the eyes, and calmly said, "No, I haven't; I follow the rules." I still stayed quiet, but inside, I was reeling, thinking about how the day before I was listening to rap in her egregiously large SUV, with her behind the wheel talking on her cell phone while she weaved in and out of traffic and went well over the speed limit. Mind you, I had no problems riding around in her truck, bumping DMX tracks; I had a problem with her lying.

It was at that moment she lost the student. The reason why?

As humans, we can only learn from those who are imperfect; we can't learn from those who are perfect.

How is anyone realistically supposed to strive for perfection?

The student knew my boss was lying and trying to put on the front of being a "model citizen" to prove her point. So he checked out of the conversation and just sat there shaking his head and saying, "Okay" every once in awhile. Gone was any possibility of having a teachable moment with this student.

Even if my boss had responded with, "Yeah, I have done things that were wrong; I just wasn't dumb enough to get caught," we would have been in a better place. But she blew her opportunity to be real with him, and in turn, she blew her opportunity to establish rapport and connect with him at a true respect-building level.

That was my boss' biggest weakness—her inability to admit when she was wrong. When her feet were to the fire, she played dumb, blamed other people, talked around it, got defensive and huffy, and would make unrelated excuses. She was anything but authentic during those times. In my mind, one of the worst reasons to behave inauthentically is to prove a point.

We cannot make someone be authentic. Only we know who our true authentic selves are. So if we try to force others to be authentic, we are probably doing it through our own lens, not theirs. In other words, we would project our idea of what we look like when we are being authentic onto others, but being authentic means being uniquely you, so that does not work. However, that does not mean that we can't have a role in helping others feel comfortable and confident in being their true genuine selves. In fact, I think it's our duty in each of our close relationships to challenge each other when we are acting or speaking in a manner that goes against our true self.

One time when I wish I had stepped up and said something was when I was a resident assistant (RA) in college. I was an RA for three full years, but the most impactful time was when I spent the summer with a group of students who were admitted to the university on a probationary basis for the summer session. In order to be fully admitted in the fall, they had to maintain a certain GPA in their summer classes, attend study hall hours, and stay out of judicial trouble. Their academic future depended on it.

Since they all had to take the same classes, go to study hall, and live in the same community-bath-style floors in the residence hall, the community became very close, very quickly. One year, in an act of camaraderie, we masking-taped nicknames onto everyone's doors.

WHO GETS TO SEE YOUR IMPERFECTIONS?

One of my residents was given the nickname "Dad." You might picture that the person with that nickname would be the fun police on the floor—a guy who walked around in slippers and a bathrobe, making sure everyone was completing his or her math homework before a dynamic dinner conversation about mutual funds and an evening of documentaries. Truth be told, though, "Dad" was an acronym for "Drunk Ass Dan."

One night, I was hanging out in my residence hall room when I heard, from down the hall, a lot of grumbling and "shh-ing." When I pushed my rolling chair outside my door to see what was going on, I observed two of my residents walking down the hall with Dan slumped over their shoulders. The two alert students saw me, said, "Oh, crap, it's James!," chucked Dan onto his bed, and took off running because "I didn't see them." Naturally, the functioning, running students weren't my concern at that time, so I went to check on Dan post-abandonment.

I went into Dan's room and found him sitting, eyes closed, on his bed, leaning against the wall. I asked whether he would mind if I sat down with him. He made an undecipherable noise, which I took, optimistically, for agreement. After sitting down with him, I tried talking to him in an attempt to figure out whether he was okay and what had happened. It was obvious he was not doing well. I asked him what he had been drinking, where he had been, etc. At this point, it was only around 9:45 p.m. so I believed it was too early for him or anyone to be *this* intoxicated. I was wrong. I found out later from the two students who "dropped" him off that they had discovered him sitting in a bush after they had watched him yell at a manhole cover. Apparently, he had also fallen off a low tree branch earlier that evening.

Dan didn't respond coherently to any of my questions. Instead, he leaned on me while mumbling. Then he fell on me in such a manner that by the end of our "conversation," I was holding Dan like a giant baby in my lap. I, again, tried to ask him some questions. This time, he responded with an assertive, "MOM WAFFLES MORNING SCHOOL!" Turns out, he was hallucinating in my arms. A few moments later, he passed out, so I laid him down on his rug on his side.

I then paced around his room for what felt like fifteen minutes, but it was probably only two. I did not know what to do. RA emergency protocol is pretty clear in situations like these—I should call the police immediately to get him medical attention and then call my supervisor. I was scared to make those phone calls, though; if I made those calls, Dan would not be able to go to college in the fall, so I knew I would be taking that away from him.

I was always the super-easy-going RA who focused more on building a community than throwing the code of conduct at people. I preferred to have conversations with my residents, telling them to be smarter about their actions, versus documenting their misbehaviors and sending them through the school's judicial process. So calling the police on Dan and ruining his hopes of being fully admitted to the college he really wanted to attend was a moral-testing moment.

I opted to call my friend, Melissa, who was not an RA, to tell her what was going on. She assertively told me, "Call the cops, you idiot." That was the slap I needed to bring me back to reality. I thanked her and promptly called the police. They arrived alongside the paramedics; it wound up taking three smelling salts to wake up Dan. When he came to, they gave him a breathalyzer, and he blew a 0.375 Blood Alcohol Content (BAC). A 0.08 BAC in most states is the legal limit, and a 0.40 BAC is brain dead.

The police told me I had probably saved Dan's life that night; truthfully, I felt like crap. I didn't feel bad because I hesitated to make the phone call, though. I felt bad that I had done nothing up to that point to help Dan stop his self-destructive behaviors.

Right when he became "Drunk Ass Dan," why had I not pulled him aside and talked to him? Why hadn't I asked him:

"So, is your nickname going to be DAD for the next four, or probably more like five or six years of college with a nickname like that? Dan, did you choose this nickname, or was it chosen for you and you like how it feels? Are you living up to your nickname because you think that's what other people want you to do, or is it your choice? Are you being true to your authentic self or just to a reputation?

Maybe if I had taken the time to ask those questions, I could have stopped his downward spiral much sooner. Maybe I could have prevented him from putting himself in a near-death situation. Maybe he would have been able to attend college that fall. Alas, I didn't challenge him with those questions.

We all likely have someone in our lives like Dan. There are "Dans" in our families and friend-groups, at our work, in our organizations, in our places of worship, on our teams. It's time to step up and be that good friend, relative, or teammate and have the tough conversation we know will initially be met with defensiveness. Or maybe we are

Dan. Maybe we need someone to find the courage to speak to us and call us out in a loving manner.

We see similar situations play out in our personal lives all of the time. Remember the last time you went through a breakup, and all of a sudden, people came out of the woodwork to say things like, "Good for you; you deserve better," or "I never liked her or him for you," or "You seemed happy, but I never understood why," or "You were a different person when he or she was around." Where were all of those "friends" during the relationship? Don't you wish they had said something sooner? Would it have caused you to question your relationship if they had?

My buddy Mike was dating a girl in college who, while a perfectly fine human being, was not, in my opinion, right in the long run for him. After giving her a chance and spending a weekend with them as a couple, I had the opportunity to speak to Mike alone. Mike was driving me back to the airport and asked me what I thought about her. I told him honestly, "Keep having fun with her if you guys are enjoying each other's company, but you're not going to marry her." I just did not see it. Between the frustrating stories he had already shared about her and not hearing the excitement that only being in love can bring to someone's voice, I just had this feeling, and I cared enough about him and our relationship to share my honest thoughts with him. Mike was quiet after I shared my opinion with him, so I was nervous that maybe I had said too much. Putting your opinion out there in those moments is risky. If the other person knows you genuinely care about her and you bring it up from a point of concern rather than from a judgmental place, it helps a lot. In Mike's case, their relationship ran its course, and after they broke up, he thanked me for giving him some perspective.

At the end of the day, people must be real and have the courage to challenge others to be real, too. That is where the idea of leading by example shines through and the idea of perfection must be shot down. Leaders who try to separate every facet of their lives, as if each one is able to stand alone without the others, are projecting an impossible life. Your mind, body, and spirit are present at work, at home, during your hobbies, in your health, and they are all connected. People who are trying to convey perfection in one or more of these facets of life are likely dropping the ball in another.

It is critical for all leaders to allow themselves to be human. The moment we start to prioritize our image over anything else is the moment we start to lose at life. Be real around those who follow you so they can see a realistic path to success. We cannot place expectations on others that we ourselves cannot live up to. Time and energy are limited resources, and if we expect others around us to have more than we do of either, then we are being unjust and poor role models.

As you consider this chapter's points, think about some of these questions: What version of yourself do you allow others to see? What defense mechanisms do you have in place, and do they protect you from yourself or others? Have you been avoiding having any hard conversations with friends or coworkers? It's time for us to start focusing on owning who we are so we can show others the real us. If Kanye West can admit to being self-conscious, I feel the rest of us can give it a shot, too. Being comfortable in one's own skin, thoughts, and actions is a lifelong process, but it's time to start putting in the work.

CHAPTER 5
DO YOU LEAD WITH LOVE?

Give Up Your Heart.

I want to talk about love, vulnerability, and how it relates to leadership and building loyalty. But first, a little background:

Over the past six years, I have had the honor to officiate some of my friends' weddings. Talk about a nerve-wracking job! As a professional speaker, I have stood and talked before audiences of over 2,000 people, but I am always most nervous when I officiate at a wedding. You can't mess that up; it's only happening once...hopefully. If I did mess it up, not only would I be ruining the most special day in my friends' lives, but I would also have to deal with the bride's parents and older siblings who are all 6'6", have tribal tattoos, and are wearing UFC T-shirts under their suits.

Nerves aside, I love being there for my friends, and it was a true honor to perform all of their ceremonies. Quick shout out to Dorothy and Alex, Heidi and Mark, Megan and Shawn, Angela and Travis, Amanda and Eric, Christina and Jimmy, Amanda and Tom, Kaitlin and

Shawn, Justine and Marissa, and Leigh and Nick; thank you all for letting me be part of your special day!

Whenever I'm asked to officiate at a wedding, after thanking the couple approximately 461 times, I say that I would be honored to officiate, but that I have three stipulations: 1) If you want anything religious in your ceremony, please include it through your readers and/or cantors, 2) You're going to write your own, individual vows, but I will help you, and 3) We are going to meet up at least two or three times prior to the wedding to talk about your relationship.

The first stipulation is fairly straightforward: I am not a "man of the cloth," nor will I pretend to be. Truth be told, I was ordained on the church of the Internet—which is eerily easy to do. I respect any beliefs you have or do not have, but it is not my place to "throw in" some religious points and jargon when I, quite literally, would not practice what I preach.

The second stipulation is my way of strongly suggesting that the couple think critically about their feelings for each other and their upcoming life together. Typically, when a couple shares the first draft of their vows with me, the word "love" is all over it. While I appreciate the word, and I see how it fits in the given context, after a while, "love" becomes the easy thing to say; its meaning becomes casual and clipped.

In life, there are a bunch of what I call, "Okay, I love you. Bye" moments. For example, when we get off of the phone, or when we're leaving for work. I understand the idea behind a quick, "Okay, I love you. Bye," but what if we never get to see that person again? I want to know that I said not just, "I love you" before I lost that person but *why* I love him or her so the person always knows it, and so I can have a little more peace of mind.

Please recognize, I understand the quick "Okay, I love you. Bye" moments. No matter how long we talk, if my parents don't say, "I love you" back to me before we get off the phone, then I'm staying on the phone. We probably say, "Okay. Take care. I love you," about forty-seven times before one of us hangs up, and I am fine with that. The idea of my parents passing, never having known how much I value and respect them, how much I appreciate everything they have done for me, and how to me they are individually inspirational mentors and together phenomenal parents, scares the shit out of me. But here's the thing.... Why don't I say any of those things at any other time during the conversation?

How about you? Do you regularly say why you love someone in conversation instead of just the shorthand, "I love you"?

Have you ever seen those pills that have the clear casing with all of the little balls inside? In my mind, that's what the word "love" is. Love is that casing, and all of the little balls inside are the hundreds of real emotions about how we feel about that person. We say, "love," when we could say, "You make my heart smile" or "You motivated me to be a better person." We say, "love," when we could say, "Thank you for being patient with me; I know I can be weird sometimes, but you make me feel accepted when I need it most." If we rattled off all of these things every time we got off the phone, it would be excessive. That's where the word "love" comes in very handy because rather than being like "Okay, babe; I'm off to work, youmakemefeellikel-'mabettermanworthyofrespectandIthinkyou'rethemostwonderfully supportivewomanIcouldhaveeverfoundthankyouforbeinginmylifeIthinkyou'regoingtobeanamazingmothertoourchildrenandwowInev-erknewIcouldfeelthisgood, take care!", we just have to say, "Okay, I'm off to work. Love you!"

But the problem comes in when we always hide behind that "love casing." When you say the word "love" *and* you *mean* it, you should feel vulnerable.

That is why I make the couple whose wedding I am officiating break down and explain what exactly they mean when they say, "I love you." And let's be honest; if you can't put it all out on the table on your wedding day, then it's time to rethink what you're getting yourself into. In order truly to love someone else, we have to allow ourselves to be vulnerable.

And now we've arrived at my third stipulation for officiating at someone's wedding: the couple must agree to meet with me two or three times to talk about their relationship.

During my pre-marriage conversations with couples, I ask them to discuss how communication flows between them—both in times when they are happy as clams, and in times when they are so upset that they want to shove bullfrogs into each other's mouth. I also ask them to reflect on how they show love to the other person using Gary Chapman's *The Five Love Languages*. (I've heard it is an awesome book, though I only read the part I needed at the time, but if you're a reader, I totally recommend it. Go to http://www.5lovelanguages. com/ to learn what your love language is and more about Mr. Chapman's book!)

One important concept Mr. Chapman emphasizes is that sometimes the way we show our love is not always the way our partner knows how to receive it (or wants to receive it). For example, if you are someone who needs to hear "I love you" from your partner through regular verbal affirmation, but instead, your partner shows his or her love to you through acts of service like making the coffee in the morning or ironing your clothes, you may not readily perceive those actions as love; you expect to hear it—not be shown it. Learning how each of you likes to receive and show love is something couples do not often think about, but knowing this detail about yourself and your partner is a super-easy way to frame your expectations and, in turn, boost your communication. It's cliché to say that good communication is the key behind every successful relationship, but clichés become clichés for a reason: they are stupidly correct.

So, if the foundation of great relationships is communication, then the keystone of great communication is vulnerability. In order actually to love someone, you have to be vulnerable. Which is why this chapter begins with the quote, "Give Up Your Heart." BOOM! DONE! Great chapter, everyone! Just kidding!

So which comes first: vulnerability or love?

First off, there are different types of love: parent-child, sibling-sibling, friend-friend, and partner-partner, just to name a few. Vulnerability has to be experienced in all of these relationships in order for the love to last. If there is not some sense of vulnerability, then love can be taken for granted and individuals will be left feeling unfulfilled, as if something is missing. Love is like a game of catch—you can't do it by yourself. You can't control what's going to happen on the other end, so all you can do is throw the ball and trust that the other person truly wants to catch it.

In my opinion, between love and vulnerability, the hints of love come first. I think love is when we're looking at the person and we get a little lump in our throats, or when you are apart and you remember something the person said to you or the way he or she looked at you, and you get goose-bumps, butterflies, or warm fuzzies. But I think vulnerability comes very quickly thereafter, and unless it's avoided and pushed into the depths of your pinky toe, it allows you to be *in* love.

Love and vulnerability have a cinnamon-bun-like relationship. A cinnamon bun without the sugary-cinnamony-goodness is just a bland pastry with nothing to look forward to. Love without vulnerability, though safe, is boring, predictable, and gets old very quickly. Vulnerability allows you to live in the moment and appreciate the full weight of love. On the other hand, a cinnamon bun without any pastry has no substance, no backbone: it's too much flavor with nothing stable. Vulnerability without love is too risky and terrifying; you need something to grab on to and trust. So the two spiral together and infuse one another to create an amazingly surreal experience, which is often unbelievable, for all of those involved.

"Hey, James," you might be saying by now, "thanks for the lecture on love. When can I expect the cheesy, stuffed bear holding an 'I love you' heart? I thought this was a book on leadership, but now I have the urge to watch *Love Actually* with a tub of ice cream." All right, friends; calm down and put your tissues and fuzzy slippers away. That section was for my fellow emotional "feelers." Here is a little something more concrete for all of my more pragmatic friends.

You need to know how and when to be vulnerable and love if you're ever going to know how to lead effectively.

DO YOU LEAD WITH LOVE?

Think about it: If you are running a company that is doing very well and hitting all of its financial goals, but the people around you feel more like drones than partners, you might be considered a great manager. You might even be able to consider yourself a successful businessperson, but you are not a true *leader*.

Whereas, if you cultivate the idea that everyone plays a critical role in the team's success and you make members feel that through positive affirmation and well-thought-out feedback, individuals will take notice and feel appreciated and heard; then, your team will have a greater sense of positive obligation to keep putting in good work for the betterment of the organization. That is being a leader.

Now, as I said earlier, love comes in all shapes and forms. A supervisor doesn't show love by whispering sweet nothings into a coworker's ear or by calling an employee up late at night just to say, "Hi" and talk because she was thinking about her. Instead, supervisors show love through their investment in individuals and by recognizing the growth potential of their followers. They cultivate their followers' strengths and recognize their contributions to the team's overall success or end goal. Leaders can't do that if they are not emotionally invested in their followers' potential. But if leaders can show that they are actively engaged and concerned with their employees' development, then, I believe, that is the exact time when loyalty is developed.

Loyalty is a scary word for the "commitophobes" out there, but it is a critical component to any leader-follower relationship. Building loyalty goes far beyond finding and following the alpha—though it would be delightfully entertaining to watch two people in suits square off against each other between the cubicles and run at each other full speed to see who is the strongest. Sadly, that would just lead to concussions, lawsuits, and awkward grunting—not loyalty. To build your team's trust, three key components are needed:

competency, authentic interactions, and love.

Competency is first. In the words of Steve Martin, "be undeniably good." You can only feign competence for so long before you're outed like a manatee at the whale party. You have to know what you're talking about when you are leading others. Otherwise, they will see you as incompetent and either resent you, seek ways to backstab you, or intentionally keep you out of the loop to make you seem even less intelligent. As you learned earlier, I love to try to fit in everywhere. I paratrooper my way into conversations I probably have no place being in, but I do not do that in my work. When it comes to leadership development, working with college students, and personally motivating those around me, I speak articulately and accurately. If your employees or team members see that you know what you're talking about, they will respect and trust you more.

The second component to developing loyalty is to interact with those around you authentically. I can usually tell within seconds of speaking with someone whether he is trying to be someone he is not. Feel free to save the humble brags, credentialing, and the like for your social media persona. When interacting with someone, the more transparent you are, the better. A lot of this goes back to what Simon Sinek says: "People don't buy what you do; they buy why you do it." The more people understand the "why" behind your expectations, the more likely they are to get on board. On top of that, the "why" must be apparent in your own actions as well; otherwise, you're just sitting in an obnoxious parent-like "because I told you so" moment. Your words and actions must be congruent—that means not just saying, "Oh, yeah, I've made tons of mistakes." It means sharing your story and being acutely interested in theirs.

Love is the final component. Love equals a leader's investment in the growth of her followers both inside and outside of work. Professional development should not just be a benefit that employees receive; it should be an organizational culture. I carefully choose the word "love" rather than "develop" because when we love someone, we have a sense of responsibility for that person and where he or she is going. Parents do more than develop their children; they are invested in the entire process. Leaders must show that they care deeply about their followers' lives; they do that by being present during times of need and pushing when opportunities for growth appear.

I use the word "invest" a lot in this chapter. Let me be clear about what I think "investing" in others looks like. Time is the most valuable commodity we humans have. Investment means spending time with those on our team to ensure they are: receiving praise where deserved, hearing articulate critical feedback, being actively listened to, and being respected as fellow human beings who have lives outside of the office.

When I supervised my staff, part of my job description was to make sure they were doing their jobs; but if I focused only on that—meeting expectations—we would have all been unfulfilled. I had individual meetings with each of my staff members to discuss not only work, but to get to know them and their stories as well. Inevitably, by the end of the year, we would break down every facet of their lives to talk about what was working and what was not. By taking this extra step, I knew when one of them was dealing with a parent who needed extra care, or when one of them was just starting a relationship, or when one of them felt as though he or she was not cut out for the job. Creating a space where each staff member and I could discuss each of these situations allowed our relationship to deepen, reconfirmed my investment in each one as a person, and served as a catalyst in the person's own work performance. But if all I talked about was job performance and I never invested in them as individuals, then I likely would not have had the same impact, and ultimately, I would have been an ineffective supervisor. Instead...

I created an environment where my staff members knew I cared about them as people first and as employees second.

I refused to let my employees call their positions "jobs." Jobs are places you begrudgingly show up to every day, do what you're supposed to do, and leave. Instead, I told them to call their positions "experiences." I needed my staff to see there was so much more to their positions than what was listed in their job descriptions. So I loved them by dedicating our time together to their growth both personally and professionally. In return, they became fiercely loyal, and together, we became a force to be reckoned with.

It is time to give up your heart. If we don't love as leaders, then our followers/employees/coworkers will feel like they are only showing up to work, not showing up to be part of something bigger. It takes vulnerability to admit to yourself and others that you cannot do it alone. While it may be scary at first, if you surround yourself with competent individuals who will you love back and communicate with you authentically, then you'll find yourself at the head of a fiercely loyal tribe, eager to bring your vision to life.

CHAPTER 6
DO YOU LIKE THE PERSON YOU'VE BECOME?

Know the morals of your story.

Morals. What a heavy word. We all react differently when we hear it. Some people get lumps in their throats. Some look away, while others start talking about Catholic guilt. A few get excited, but most slowly shift to a defensive stance. My simplified meaning of the word "morals" is: your own personal definition of what is right and what is wrong. How you get to your own definition is up to you. Maybe it's passed down from your parents and teachers, maybe it's influenced by your faith, or maybe it's based on your own life experiences, through trial and error.

No matter how you learned to define what is right and what is wrong, it is your own moral compass that now informs the choices, judgments, and actions you make. Yes, our morals will be tested and tweaked, but they should not be compromised. Let me ask you a very simple question: "Do you like the person you've become?" Marinating on this question forces you to think about whether you have ever compromised your morals.

A quick analogy: I think we as people are like brick pillars. Stick with me here. Every brick in our pillar is a different experience we have had. For example:

- Learning how to ride a bike
- Getting the ice cream truck to stop for the first time
- Your first kiss
- Your first breakup
- The first fancy dinner you ever ate
- Dealing with the death of loved ones
- Meeting your role model and/or mentors
- Getting into college
- Being cheated on
- Getting the job you really want
- Watching that guy get punched in the face and realizing you never want to get punched in the face

This is obviously a short list of potential experiences we have all shared. All are valuable experiences, each one a different brick in our pillar. But our morals make up the mortar that holds all of those experiences together and allows us to stand tall as individuals; without them, we are just loose piles of bricks.

Our morals are shaped by every experience we have. Without our morals, we could be someone who is manipulated by others' opinions and convinced to act in ways we aren't proud of. We all know someone like that, right? You know, that person who has no backbone and is constantly flip-flopping his beliefs because he doesn't know who he is yet?

DO YOU LIKE THE PERSON YOU'VE BECOME?

I have had a lot of conversations with people in the dating pool about this situation. Having a deep desire to be in a relationship is a very dangerous place to be. Sure, the company sounds great, and maybe all of your friends are in relationships, but what is the price you are willing to pay for settling? Serial daters, people who never seem to be single for more than a week, are examples of people who haven't learned how to be themselves yet.

There is a telltale sign of individuals who need to focus on being more centered in their own lives. Rather than going through sometimes painful and time-consuming self-reflection, they seek others who appear stable to hold them up and make them feel better about themselves. These individuals, rather than focusing on strengthening their own brick pillars by analyzing what's important to them and what they feel is right, lean on others' pillars. That's why, when the relationship ends, their lives comes crashing down while the other person can move on more quickly.

We must develop the ability to be our own barometer of self-worth. Defining ourselves based on the company we keep or the relationship we are in is a beautiful way to avoid owning the kind of person we are and to evade making decisions based on our own definition of happiness. The stronger we are morally, however, the less likely we are to find ourselves in these compromising relationships.

Taking time to reflect on who we are and what our values are is a tedious but imperative process. It is why journaling, personal blogging, and silent retreats are very healthy. A lot of times, we don't realize our behaviors are unhealthy. We are just going through life and repeating patterns that seem to have worked in the past, so why change them?

LEADING IMPERFECTLY

I'll share a personal story with you that I'm not exactly proud of. From seventh grade until my sophomore year in college, I had a huge stealing problem. Before I go any further, please know that I wasn't out holding up banks, doing carjackings, or pickpocketing. Truth be told, I was a chocoholic and had a serious addiction for anything made by Reese's.

It started in seventh grade when I would steal pretzel rods and Little Debbie Nutty Bars from the middle school cafeteria. Seventh grade was the only time I ever got caught, but instead of that deterring me from doing it again, I knew I just needed to get better at it. From there on out, I never got caught, and I kept doing it because I told myself, "Well, if you're good at something...."

I continued to steal straight through my first couple of years of college. In my undergrad years, I would walk into the convenience store on campus with cargo shorts on and have a conversation with the cashier while I was slipping candy bars into my pockets. My roommates knew about my unfortunate hobby, so every once in awhile, I would get them their favorite candy and call it a "no-tell tax." Again, I am not proud of this; I am just sharing my truth with you. The fact of the matter is that I was in a pattern. A pattern for which I had never been punished and only enjoyed the benefits.

Then, one day in my sophomore year, I was at my favorite electronics store in Wilmington when I saw that the speakers I had had my eye on for the past few months were on sale. I remember it was President's Day, and the sale was only going on that weekend.

My sophomore year, I was a resident assistant on campus and got paid every other week. Unfortunately, this was an off week, and I had already spent my last check, so I couldn't afford my dream speakers. So I did what any privileged college student would do in that moment—I called my parents.

I explained to my father my conundrum and asked whether he would be willing to forward me some money. He thought about it for a minute and responded, "Yes." I could not believe it; I was so excited! But then he kept talking. He said he would buy me the speakers, but I had to do him a favor.... I had to stop stealing.

I knew my father was aware that I had stolen a few things here and there, but I didn't think he knew the extent of my illegal hobby. So I first thought to myself, *Who told Dad?* Alas, that didn't matter; Dad knew. So I responded to him with a hesitant, "Okay."

He continued, "James, the man you are is not congruent with a person who has a stealing problem. You have such a great reputation on campus; why are you doing something that could ruin it? When your mother and I come to visit you at college, we love meeting all of the people you have had a positive impact on. Sometimes, one of your friends or residents pulls us aside and tells us how you helped him through a rough time in his life, or helped him get an on campus job, or just how when he sees you around campus, you reassure him that he is where he is supposed to be.

"Also," my dad continued, "when you introduced us to your Vice Chancellor, she pulled us aside and thanked us for letting the university borrow you for five years. She said you were one of the best community builders on campus and someone who really gets what the student experience is about. She also told us that you were one of the few students she invited to be a part of one of her committees."

My dad finished by saying, "No one we spoke to about you mentioned anything about your stealing. They didn't finish by saying, 'Oh, and your son also grabs me a bag of Skittles every once in awhile, so that's awesome, too!' So, James,

> "Why are you doing something that if anyone found out about it, would immediately make them question what they thought about you?"

Damn.

My dad was right.

Where did my stealing fit into my moral fabric? Why was I doing something that would ruin everything else that I stood for? Why was I doing something I wasn't ultimately proud of?

But that's the thing; we all have a little something we do that we think if others found out about, would make them take pause or have to take a step back. Hopefully, it's not illegal; if so, just go ahead and cut it out of your life now. This is not limited to things we do when others are not looking, however.

It also includes the things you say around like-minded individuals about people who are different from you. It includes the internal thoughts you have about people who are a different race, sexual orientation, religion, or gender than you. Sorry to report this, but we all have biases. That includes you, person who "doesn't see color," or who "has one gay friend," or who uses the phrase, "Bless his heart" or "No offense," right before you point out something different about someone.

Do those thoughts align with your moral compass? If not, then it's time to check yourself and own those biases so you can begin to work on removing them from your brain and speech patterns. When we don't, we are doing others and ourselves a huge disservice. We carry unnecessary weight, unproductive hate, and hurtful stereotypes toward others.

Authentic leaders are not perfectly moral individuals.

But every decision authentic leaders make gets filtered through their morals first. That may mean they have to make unpopular decisions. But it also means they go to bed every night with a clearer conscience and less guilt on their shoulders.

Plenty of examples exist of the leaders of companies revisiting their morals and changing the way they do business. One of the more recent examples was when CVS announced it would no longer carry any tobacco products in its stores. This decision was definitely a bold and profit-effecting move, but when asked about it, CVS CEO Larry J. Merio stated, "Ending the sale of cigarettes and tobacco products at CVS/pharmacy is the right thing for us to do for our customers and our company to help people on their path to better health," and concluded with, "Put simply, the sale of tobacco products is inconsistent with our purpose."

I love that statement. The company's firm decision models authentic leadership at its finest because in selling tobacco, it was doing something that did not align with its morals or what was right for its customers. Also, let's be honest.... This move is not going to make CVS broke. It is doing just fine.

Morals in business often get fuzzy because, at the end of the day, money has to be made; otherwise, there is no business. That is where the idea of "purpose" comes in. Your purpose, or the reason behind why you do what you do, can have multiple aspects, but the minute we take our morals out of the equation is the minute we begin failing.

CVS provides a great example for us all to learn from. As leaders of organizations and teams, we are sometimes faced with hard decisions. The most popular decision is not always the best decision; often short-term praise or income is often chased over long-term success. That is why all decisions must be siphoned through our morals.

What are the morals of your story? The minute we start compromising our definition of what is right and what is wrong is the same moment we start to destroy the person we are. We demolish our brick pillars, but for what? A Like? A retweet? A dollar? A potential partner? If that's the kind of person you are, then allow me to ask, again: "Do you like the person you've become?"

CHAPTER 7
ARE YOU A ROLE MODEL OR A HERO?

You are allowed to be human.

Most young leaders I know spend a lot of their time trying to help everyone. They double-book themselves. They have not learned the meaning of the word "No," and in turn, they consistently put others' needs before their own. What winds up happening are two things: 1) the followers don't see any progress so they begin to show up less and less, and 2) the leader gets burnt out, beats herself up, and is convinced she is not cut out to be a leader.

It is impossible to be everything for everyone. If someone looks like he is, he is probably faking it.

As a student leader, I made this same mistake—I was faking it. I was overcommitted, never said, "No," rarely slept, gained weight, and let my academics suffer. I wanted to be there for everyone. That included my role as a student leader: as a resident assistant (RA), I was there for everyone on my floor at all hours, and I was ready to talk with them about whatever for as long as they needed. My schedule didn't matter, and what my body was telling me mattered even less.

My supervisor, Michelle, pulled me aside after I had repeated this pattern a few times. She told me to look at my life as if it were a pie. You already know I love desserts, so I was quickly onboard with this idea. She said, "Cut your pie so each slice represents an accurate percentage of how much time you devote to it weekly. Include sleep, studying, time spent with your partner, social life, eating, all of the clubs you're involved in, and being an RA." When I finished, I had a lot of small pieces of pie; my pie looked more like a bicycle wheel. Michelle then asked me, "Is it fair that each of these commitments only gets a small percentage of your energy and time?" Truth was, it was not.

My inability to say, "No," and thus my over-commitment to too many things, was actually the primary reason why my college girlfriend wanted to break up with me. She and I dated for a little over two years in college, and we were both very involved student leaders. I was just *very* very involved. And on top of that, I am what some might call an "includer." My philosophy is, "Why hang out with one or two people when you can invite everyone?" As a result, it was rare that she ever got time with just me. She told me she did not feel like she was a priority in my life, and the truth was, she was not. Don't get me wrong; of all the people to whom I devoted my time, she got the most, but I devoted my time to *a lot* of people. So while her piece of my "pie" was bigger than others' pieces, it was, understandably, not big enough.

My desire in college to be there for and with everyone, not just my girlfriend, came from a deeper place. My self-esteem in high school was very low. Fortunately, I was good at faking it by being the loud funny guy, but I had some serious lows during that time. When I was alone at home and no one would call me to hang out, I thought it must be because no one actually liked me. I would think that while they laughed at my jokes in school, they did not want to spend time with me and get to know me. Some days, I thought if I died, no one would show up to my funeral. I never thought about whether or how I would commit suicide, but I remember thinking no one would care if I were gone. Those were some dark times.

In college, I got to be more of the person I always knew I was, and I was shown a lot of love for it. I knew tons of people, and tons of people knew me, and I loved that. I would walk down the center of campus and pass out high-fives and ask, "How ya doin'?" left and right. I was the first runner-up for homecoming king one year. (I lost to a kid who campaigned for it.... I'm not bitter...anymore.) I was frequently late to class, but it didn't matter to me. I would get out of tickets on campus because the campus police loved me and knew how valuable I was in the residence halls. I could walk up to basically any nightclub in town, skip the line, and walk right in. I frequently got free meals in the dining hall and rarely signed in when I visited my friends in other residence halls...including my girlfriend's all-female building. I regularly met with the upper administrators on campus because they valued my thoughts. Lastly, my senior year, I was named "Man of the Year" on campus. Okay, now I'll get over myself, but I promise there is a take-home behind listing all those points.

College was an awesome five years for me. Yes, five years. There's no shame in a victory lap. My favorite student leader position was being an RA. I did it for three years and five summer sessions, and I would still be doing it today if I could convince my wife to live in a residence hall room with me and share a twin extra-long mattress.

As an RA, I would stay up to whatever hour of the night just to hang out with my residents. The school I went to was right by the Atlantic Ocean, so at least one night a week, someone would say, "Let's stay up and go watch the sunrise!" I never discouraged this idea. A couple of residents and myself would go, watch the sunrise, come back, and be first in line at the dining hall when it opened, then go back to the residence hall, and...get ready for our 9 a.m. classes...right? No. I would *say* I was getting ready for class, but I would really just fall into my bed and turn my alarm off. My residents would frequently remark, "James, we never see you doing any work; when do you get all of your schoolwork done?" I would respond, "I get my work done after you guys go to bed!" This was a lie. I went to bed after they went to bed.

It was great for my residents because I was always there for them. We always had super-tight-knit communities, and they looked up to me. They would come to me when they had an interview they were nervous about, after they lost a loved one, if they wanted a restaurant recommendation for a date, if they were homesick, for outfit advice, and if they were thinking about hurting themselves. Whenever residents would come to my room, I would stop everything and sit on my unbelievably comfortable green couch with them and listen for as long as they wanted. It was great for them, but, in hindsight, not for me.

One thing RAs are told constantly is to remember they are students first and RAs second. RAs are also told to remind their residents of the same thing: the primary reason they are at college is to get an education, so everything else is secondary. We've all heard the phrase "Practice what you preach." Well, I certainly preached what I was supposed to, but I definitely did not practice it. My GPA in college was 2.73. On top of that, my sleeping habits were atrocious, I ate like crap, and worst of all, I was a hypocrite.

What I was trying to be was a role model. I was trying to be someone people looked up to and wanted to emulate. When it came to taking care of myself, living a healthy life, and being a good student, I consistently fell short. I was so focused on being everything to everyone else that I never made time for me. All of the social notoriety was temporarily cool, but at what price?

On planes, they tell you to put your oxygen mask on before trying to assist anyone else because if you're dead, you can't help others. Harsh? Yes. True? Yes. Certainly, I am not saying I was near death because I didn't care about myself, but I am saying that I could have helped even more people had I practiced self-care.

Let's shift gears a little. I have a question for you:

What is the difference between a hero and a role model?

When I ask this question at my talks, the first answer I usually get is "a cape"...because there is one wise guy in every crowd and that's an awesome answer. As more hands go up, the replies get deeper and deeper. One of my favorite responses was from a student at the University of Akron. (I asked him to come up to me after the keynote so I could give him credit for it; alas, he did not.) The student described the difference between a hero and a role model like this: "Hero: wrong place, wrong time, right person. Role Model: right place, right time, right person." Another answer I hear from time to time and love is: "Heroes save people; role models help people save themselves."

When I think about the difference between a hero and a role model, two concepts come to mind: tangibility and transparency. Tangibility speaks to how accessible and approachable someone is. People who are tangible are not afraid to be in the moment with others, to be present with them. They actually have an open-door policy; they don't just say they do and then get aggravated when you try and take advantage of it.

Transparency refers to how much of an "open book" someone is. Transparent individuals are not afraid to admit whether something is not their strength or they made a mistake. They will tell you about times when they have messed up in the past *and* what they learned from it. Transparent people are much less likely to hide, and they are also much less likely to get defensive when called out.

Typically, heroes are neither tangible nor transparent. They only show others the areas in which they are perfect. Heroes seemingly do nothing wrong, and they approach life as if their mere presence helps save the day. In our organizations, these are the people who try to do everything for the organization; they act like they are the key component in turning good to great, they take over meetings with their ideas exclusively, they jump in front of the parade, etc. Heroes rarely, if ever, admit fault when things go awry. They also do not respond well, or at all, to feedback...even if they ask for it. They intentionally keep people at a distance because it's harder for others to see their cracks or flaws from farther away. In college, I was unintentionally being a hero. I did not let a lot of people into my world, but I was more than willing to give them advice in theirs. I also pretended to be great in all aspects of college when I was not at all.

ARE YOU A ROLE MODEL OR A HERO?

When heroes run organizations, a huge disconnect often exists between them and the people "under" them. Communication typically only flows in one direction—from the top down. The other organization members may feel as though their ideas carry no weight. All they hear is "No." Heroes are usually of the mindset: "No one around me can do this as efficiently or effectively as I can, so let me just do it, and you're welcome, everyone else." If a hero is running the show, things may get done, but at what cost? While heroes are trying to save the day and take their organizations to the "promised land," the people around them are frustrated because they are never allowed to be involved in the organization; therefore, they have no stake in its success. Unfortunately, by the time the hero does ask for help, it's to resolve too-big of a problem, or it's too late to recapture people's energy and passion.

Role models as leaders, on the other hand, authentically lead by example and are both tangible and transparent. Tangible role model leaders are accessible. They are available for meetings and do not scoff at people seeking to speak with them. They show others that they matter by asking for help and letting their ideas carry weight in the final decision. If they disagree with someone, they do not shut that person down with a Heisman Trophy stiff arm, but rather, they talk about why they think another direction would be more successful.

Role model leaders are transparent. If they don't know the answer to a question, they will be honest about it. They will either tell the person they will get back to her with the answer in X amount of time, or they will direct her to a better resource. Role models are not afraid to talk in detail about a time when they slipped up. They allow others to learn from their mistakes and, hopefully, not succumb to the same pitfalls by sharing their stories. They also make their colleagues feel more comfortable about being human in the workplace. These two qualities take unneeded stress off the people around them.

When I was supervising my team members, I would strive to be both tangible and transparent with them. At the beginning of each academic year, I would get a new team, so I would need to establish rapport with each individual and the whole group. One thing I would do was have all of them bring a list of three things they were good at related to the RA position and three things they were less confident about. At the meeting, I would have them all share publically what they wrote. Since they had already gotten the job, I told them all to be as honest as possible and to leave their fluffy weaknesses at home (things like, "I work too much" or "I don't know how to say, 'No'" interview responses). As they shared the items they were working on, I would always ask where they thought each weakness came from. Did they just not prioritize or think about it? Were they legitimately less competent in that area? Or did they not consider it an area that was important to their success? After everyone shared, I would share as well.

I told them the things I struggle with such as organization and procrastination because I wanted them to know that everyone on our team had room to grow, including me! They needed to know none of us could be everything to everyone, but that our strengths could be something to someone else on the team.

It takes more time to be a role model than a hero because role model leadership focuses on both the development of the individuals involved *and* on getting results (getting the job done). When you focus on both pieces, as opposed to just getting results, it is an investment in the organization's long-term growth versus the short-term moment of glory. Role models recognize the value of individual growth right alongside of organizational growth. Consequently, when asked questions, they are likely to flip it back on the asker to challenge her to think critically and grow rather than just giving out answers. However, at the end of the day, role models still take responsibility for their own actions and the actions of their organizations as opposed to making excuses and pointing fingers.

By being both transparent and tangible, role models exemplify authentic leadership. They lead within their means and don't try to put on a front of awesomeness.

So how does one become a role model? Unfortunately, it's not up to you. Role models go throughout their lives making choices based on what they think is right and based on what they think is important. The person being admired does not get to determine what aspect of herself will be emulated. So that means you just have to live an authentic life. In college, I was *trying* to be a role model, but that's not how one earns that title. Heroes try; role models just are.

At some point, we need to realize that not everyone is going to "get us," and not everyone is going to like and/or understand us. But if we focus on doing the right thing and being people of good character, people will notice, and they will become self-reflective, and then we can...

Be something to someone.

So how do you know whether you are someone whom others look up to? How do you know whether you are seen as a mentor? One clue: You start getting asked questions like, "How did you get to where you are today?" and "What advice do you have for people who want to pursue your career?"

It is at that moment that we each must remember we are a human talking to another human. It is awesome being a mentor, so we should not take that role lightly. Check in with your mentee monthly. Ask her open-ended questions that drive thought rather than provide her with answers. If giving advice, try to share stories from your own journey as opposed to telling your mentee what to do. Try to share an equal number of times that you have succeeded along with times when you have slipped.

It is important always to monitor the relationship, though. A number of times, I have been a mentor to people who have really taken advantage of me. I worked with students who would monopolize my time, both during and after work hours. I never minded being called super-late at night by someone who was in crisis, but by answering every night, I was enabling people more than I was helping them. Mentors are not licensed counselors, and they should not try to be for the health of both themselves and their mentees.

Our organizations need more role models and less heroes.

We must approach being a leader from an authentic and realistic place. Practice saying, "No" by doing it once this week; then next week, say it twice. Taking charge of your own schedule starts with knowing what you can handle—do not try to be a hero! By focusing your time on a few things as opposed to trying to do everything, you will be a better role model. You are allowed to be human. You are allowed to have personal things you are working on. When was the last time you shared a specific time that you dropped the ball with someone who could benefit from hearing that story? Set up a meeting with a mentee, and share your strengths and struggles with her. If you do not have a mentee, keep being the best authentic person you can be, and open your eyes to see whom you influence. Be something to someone. Be a role model.

CHAPTER 8
WHAT'S YOUR LEGACY?

"Each day a little less living, a little more goodbye."
— John Robilotta, Jr.

This quote is the last line of a poem my father wrote in December 2006. He wrote it while he was spending time with his mother during her last couple of years with us. Here's the whole thing:

A Little More Goodbye

Each day a little after four
I walk across the street
to the nursing home
where my mother finally
has come to stay
no more worries over falls
or nights on the floor
diapered now and cared for

She looks forward to my
daily visit
asking every day what's new

I try to remember everything
that she might understand
knowing that by tomorrow
I can tell her all over again

I find myself stroking
her hair
and kissing her on the forehead
while not yet helpless
she is fading from my life

Each day she talks of sleep
late into the mornings now
and right after the evening meal
and this is how she will die
the doctor says
each day a little less living
a little more goodbye

— John Robilotta, Jr.

Your time on Earth is not unlimited. I personally don't know what's going to happen after I pass, so I am making the most of the time I have. When I do reach the finish line, I can tell you this: my funeral is going to be a party! I would love a New Orleans style jazz funeral with trombones blaring and a raucous crowd walking down the street after my casket. Whenever that happens, hopefully some people will be kind enough to say a few words about me at my post-mortem goodbye party. The question is...what will they say?

Most people want to leave a legacy that will live on long after they have passed. The way people go about creating that legacy varies.

WHAT'S YOUR LEGACY?

Some strive to be the best at a particular thing. They leave their names in the record books, on plaques, and have awards named after them. Others seek to leave physical impacts of their existence. They donate money to get their names on buildings, or they build schools where there were none before. Some invent technological advancements that enable us to do things that are bigger, faster, smaller, more efficient, greener, or stronger than ever before. Finally, some choose to let those they have interacted with pass on their impact. These are the teachers, parents, social workers, counselors, etc. who change the way their followers think, interact with others, and dream about what's possible.

For me, I live my life according to what I want to be said in my eulogy.

The choices I make, the manner in which I interact with others, and the way I determine what is right and what is wrong all coincide with what I hope someone will say at my funeral party. In the long run, I can't ultimately determine what will be said, but I can control what comes out of my mouth and whom I share my authentic self with today, and tomorrow, and all my living days.

Unfortunately, I have been to a lot of funerals. Some were celebrations of people who got to live very long lives, while others honored those whose time was taken too quickly. No matter how much time someone spent on this earth, you can tell fairly rapidly at a funeral who led an impactful life and who didn't.

Attending a funeral for someone who did not positively impact many others is one of the saddest experiences. It's uncomfortable to observe others striving to come up with stories to share about the person when there may not be many to choose from. It's uncomfortable to feel the pressure yourself when no one else is speaking up. It's uncomfortable when it seems as though many attendees are only there because it was the right thing to do. Particularly around death, I have found you can easily tell the difference between an awkward silence and a moment of introspection or remembrance. I've been to a few funerals like this, but one in particular stands out.

The head of the funeral parlor had just said some kind, but generic, things about the person who had passed. When he finished, he asked whether anyone would like to come up and say a few words. No one moved. Finally, someone stood up and shared a few, brief memories and sat back down. Again, no one moved. It was evident this was an awkward silence kind of moment—not a moment of remembrance. Next thing I knew, someone turned to me and said in full voice, "Hey, James, why don't you get up and share a few stories?"

I did have a number of memories of the deceased, but none were particularly flattering. I didn't want the few personal words I would say to be construed as rude or untimely. The stories I wound up sharing were certainly endearing idiosyncrasies that I will never forget about the person, but I really wish I had known what the person had wanted to be remembered for.

Asking, "What do you want to be remembered for?" or "What legacy do you hope to leave?" are questions we should ask anyone we know and love who is walking toward the light at the end of the tunnel. It's a hard question to ask at the time, but I think reflection is so important in the moment, and it's also important for others to hear the person's thoughts. When we're younger, we usually get asked often, "How do you want to be remembered?" or "What do you want your legacy to be?" But we're rarely asked those questions when we're older. I think it's important to ask that question throughout our lives.

Whenever you attend the funeral of someone who did not have an impact on a lot of people, you wonder whether that person lived a fulfilled life. Did she die happy or bitter? If she could have lived life differently, would she have? Does it matter how many people she impacted as long as she impacted some? During such moments, I am very introspective and ask myself, "Is this what my funeral will look like? Do I push people away from me, or do I welcome them into my life? What stories would people share about me? Would people share stories with fondness or with a 'Well, I guess someone should say something' motivation?"

My grandfather's funeral was quite the opposite of the one I described above. Hundreds of people came out to pay their respects, share stories, and be a part of the community that my grandfather had helped cultivate. He had an impressive and impactful life. Admirably, you would have never known it from speaking to him. He just did what he felt was right—he led by example.

To give you a little background, my grandfather was a United States Marine who served in the Pacific Theater of World War II. He was a police officer in the New York Police Department. He lived through and responded to subway fires, the Harlem Race riots, and even helped bring down the infamous serial killer, Son of Sam. Before he retired from the force, he had reached the impressive rank of First Deputy - Police Commissioner. He was man of God, so after retiring from the NYPD, he served his church community in almost every way. He would wake up early each Sunday to drive around the neighborhood and pick up people who could not drive themselves to Mass. He would create handmade wooden Christmas ornaments every year to donate to the church so it could sell them as a fundraiser. And, of course, he was a father. He helped raise his four children and taught them the values of being humble, having a strong work ethic, and doing the right thing.

My grandpa was an impressive man. But since he did not share his successes, it was up to others who knew him to talk about him. That's what his funeral was. His own children learned so many new things about him during the week of his passing that they never knew before. My brothers and I were in awe as we heard the stories people eagerly shared. There were no awkward silences at my grandfather's wake.

My grandpa's name was James Taylor. My full name is James Taylor Robilotta. Though my parents love the folk singer a lot, I was named after my grandfather. A lot of people at the funeral came up to me and said things like: "You were named after a great man," "He was a true role model," and "You have some big shoes to fill." They were/ are right.

We all have people whom we look up to, whom we want to emulate, whom we define success by. For me, that person is my grandpa. My grandpa is my hero. I would love for others to speak about me with as much love and respect as my grandpa is still spoken about today, years after he passed. At the end of the day, though, he and I are different people. I'm not going to do the things he did, and he and I have very different personalities. What I strive to do is get to the same ending place as him, using the lessons he modeled. I hope to have a funeral where people come to recount stories about the fun and impactful times we shared because they feel their lives were improved because I was a part of them. I want my eulogy to be an accurate, descriptive summation of the impact I made in the time

I had, not a forced awkward affair. I think it's okay that I'm going to make that impact on my own terms, and not the same way my grandpa did.

I'd like to think that so far I am on my way to achieving that goal, but I need to do a better job at letting others in to show them the unpolished version of myself. If I passed away today, a lot of people would appreciate the time I took to get to know them, but in the same breath, they would probably say they didn't really know a lot about me. That just means I have work to do!

The ideas in this chapter are applicable to our roles as leaders in both the long and the short term. Not only should we approach legacy leaving from the macro, "What do I want to be said in my eulogy?" sense, but also from the micro sense. Anytime we get a new role or show up to work at a new organization, we should ask ourselves, "When I leave this role, whether to pursue a new opportunity or retire, what do I want the people here to say about me, and what do I want to be able to say I did with my time?"

How about you? What do you want said at your eulogy? Will people be there because they were obligated, or because there's no way they would miss it? If I asked ten people from different facets of your life how you make them feel, what would they say?

It's important to think about these questions now. This chapter is about life and what you're doing or not doing with it; it's not about death. Maybe death is a motivator for you—it's something you're scared of. I think death scares the unfulfilled the most. A little of that fear is healthy. It serves as a reminder to get off our butts and make something of the time we have. Because each day we get closer to what my dad said, "each day a little less living, a little more goodbye."

CHAPTER 9
DO YOU TAKE YOURSELF TOO SERIOUSLY?

"You don't have to take yourself seriously to take your job seriously."
— Chris Bruno

I have a problem with the concept of professionalism. When I hear that word, I think conformity, misogynistic, old school, the way it has always been, needlessly serious, and stuck-up. I envision the stifling of creativity and the devaluing of individuality. I see dress codes and supervisors who miss the point.

As you can tell, I am quite biased on this matter and, therefore, I'll warn you that this chapter may be a little soapbox-y. I also recognize that I am fighting an uphill battle against years of societal norms, but this is a mountain I am willing to die on.

When others hear the word professionalism, they may often think: respect, success, uniformity, maturity, a business code of ethics, etc. Merriam-Webster.com defines professionalism as: "the skill, good judgment, and polite behavior that is expected from a person who is trained to do a job well." I have no problem with Webster's description; it is where the business world has taken it that perturbs me.

My argument for this entire chapter is: It is possible to be seen as respectful and as respect-worthy, competent, and a successful leader without conforming to business norms and watering down your individuality. I told this to my great friend and fellow student affairs professional, Chris Bruno, recently. He agreed with me and said, "You don't have to take yourself seriously to take your job seriously."

I clearly love his quote. I think it speaks to how I define leadership. Leadership has nothing to do with titles, image, or power. Those who think that will get to the end alone or be burnt out along the way. In my eyes:

Leadership is connecting with others, empowering them to be their best authentic selves, and working together toward a common goal.

Let's break down that definition into its three main components.

Leadership is connecting with others. I've already talked a bunch about this point in this book. To recap: share your story and be genuinely interested in listening to others' stories. Be empathetic, but also know when and where to push someone.

Leadership is empowering others to be their best authentic selves. Sadly, empowerment is a clichéd word in both the business and educational worlds. It is a word that people just say to sound impressive because it carries weight and feels important. Like all clichés, empowerment is better in practice than when spouted out flippantly. Allow me to illustrate this with a hypothetical story:

One day, a good friend of yours and mine, Johnny, decides he wants to take a big group of us mountain climbing. Now we all know that he has been climbing mountains since he was a fetus. His mother is a climber, his grandfather was the first one to summit a number of the local peaks...so Johnny had no choice but to be a climber; it's in his blood! We agree to go because it sounds pretty awesome, and who better to go with?

Johnny is our natural leader. He has the most knowledge and experience, and the most passion. He shows up on the designated day holding a bunch of ropes and carabiners and wearing fancy climber-guy shoes. Meanwhile, the rest of us show up only holding cups of hot chocolate. It's all good, though; Johnny is our leader, and we trust him. As we start the expedition, if he wanted, Johnny could charge ahead of us all. He knows where to go, how best to navigate the pass, and he's got the right tools. He could shoot up to the top of the mountain and pull the rest of us up, but that's not what leaders do.

Leaders push; they don't pull.

If all Johnny does is pull us up, it won't be fulfilling for the rest of the team. We would all get dragged to the top, look around, take some selfies, caption them with "#mountain," and then slide back down. Whereas, if Johnny *pushes* us up the mountain while teaching us techniques, things he learned the hard way, and encouraging and applauding us, we will summit the mountain feeling like *we all* truly accomplished something. We would feel like we were a part of the mission's success.

That is my actionable definition of empowerment: leaders push; they don't pull.

Leadership is working together toward a common goal. Another word for working together is teamwork. Every successful team has players with different strengths, and that is what makes the team great. The starting five on the basketball team are not all huge seven-footers—that's not what yields the best results. You need people who can make shots from different areas of the court, and you need people who can crash the boards, block shots, pass the rock with pinpoint accuracy, and get in the way on defense.

Who do you have on your team? Hopefully, you have a mix of individuals who are good at: looking at the big picture, remembering the details, boosting morale, mediating conflict, making sales, being creative, going with the flow, and knowing when to stir the pot, You need people who are good at dreaming, doing, leading, following, and providing a strong moral compass. As their leader, it's your job to celebrate their differences, communicate their individual purposes on the team, and provide clarity for the overall vision to keep the team inspired and motivated to achieve the set goals.

While doing those three things, leaders provide articulate and timely feedback so individuals see how their actions affect the bigger picture and learn to take responsibility for upholding their pieces of the organization's mission. The best leaders then ask for the same in return so everyone is held accountable.

So what does all of that have to do with professionalism? Absolutely nothing, and therein, lies my point. Leadership is not about power. It is not about outward or inward perfection. It is not about what you are wearing. It is not about what has always been done. It is not about keeping the office at a library-like volume level. Leadership is simply about connecting, empowering, and working together.

DO YOU TAKE YOURSELF TOO SERIOUSLY?

Let's talk dress codes. Does the suit make the man? Does the man make the suit? Successful men wear suits so women should, too, if they want the same respect...right? Sadly, that is accurate right now in the business world. What about individuals who do not come from privileged backgrounds but are trying to make it in the business world? Should we count individuals like that out because they do not dress the part?

Here's my take—as long as you look like you generally care about your appearance and hygiene, I will respect the words exiting your mouth just as much as I would respect the same words coming from someone in a suit. One's ability to carry oneself with poise and confidence does not magically occur upon donning formal business attire. When we micromanage people about the way they dress, we are saying, "Conform or get out." That is simply not healthy for team-building and office morale.

Please note: Just because I do not agree with rigid dress codes does not mean I think people can come to work looking like a hot mess. It is important to be respectful of your clients and coworkers, so maybe leave the sweatpants and 1986 Grateful Dead Tour shirt with the holes in it for your personal life.

Where does laughter fit in with being a professional?

As you know, I come from a comedy background. I started doing stand-up and improv during my undergraduate years. Before that, I was the wise-butt in the back of chemistry class, cracking witty jokes about the periodic table of elements. I grew up watching the Marx Brothers, Sid Caesar, Tracy Ullman, Rodney Dangerfield, Goofy, Monty Python, *The Simpsons*, *Saturday Night Live*...you get the point.

I do not know how *not* to be funny; humor is my life! But I feel the need to subdue those comedic instincts in professional settings.

As a speaker, I am most nervous speaking to professionals. Corporate audiences simply do not laugh as much. My fellow student affairs professionals do not laugh as much, either. As a speaker, laughter provides me with two very important things: it makes me feel validated, and it shows me the audience is engaged.

So why don't those specific audiences laugh? I will take the self-esteem hit and say maybe not all of my jokes and asides are worthy of an uproarious guffaw, but I honestly do not think that is the biggest issue. I think we, as employed adults, are trained to believe that laughter does not equal professionalism. We are taught, whether consciously or sub-consciously, that being professional means curbing your emotions to remain as even-keeled as possible.

That is why whenever I give a speech to professionals, after I say a couple of funny things that get polite chuckles, I pause my presentation and give the audience permission to laugh. I give the audience permission to be present with me emotionally. Because if people feel like they cannot laugh as loud as they want, they also probably feel like they cannot express other emotions as fully as I want them to.

Being emotional does not equal being unprofessional.

Outside of laughter, being overly concerned about professionalism stifles people's stories. It forces everyone to conform and get in line. Our backgrounds, places where we struggled, times we succeeded, experiences we had, people we have met, and the fact that we love puppies and chai lattes all no longer matter. We cannot forget about the growth we have gone through in the name of professionalism.

I find that the people who outwardly take themselves the most seriously are frequently the most insecure. I once worked for a man who demonstrated that truth; he put a lot of effort into making sure others knew he had his doctorate and that he was only to be called by his title and his last name. Only a select few got to call him by his first name, Rick.

One time I was working with an off-campus vendor and needed to get a contract signed by Rick so we could move forward with the student event. The vendor sent the contract over, and it had one line for someone to sign-off on. I did not pay any attention to this and brought it to the two people who needed to approve it. The first person signed on the line; then I brought it to Rick. He looked at the contract and said, "Where am I supposed to sign this?" I told him he could sign anywhere on that page. He told me he would not sign it because there was no line for his name. Rick further said that I needed to contact the vendor and tell it to print up a new contract with two signature lines for his and the other person's name.

Because it does not have to, the vendor did not know about the inner processes/bureaucratic nature of how contract dealings worked on the campus. But now I had to call the vendor's representative, tell her what had happened, get a new contract issued, and get both signatures on it, again. All of this was because of ego. Rick took himself too seriously, and he did not see how his self-centered actions were impacting so many other people or the event's potential success. If your need to be respected and seen as a consummate professional impedes getting business done, then it is an issue.

When we allow our insecurities to drive our actions, we do not allow ourselves to see the bigger picture. We turn inward rather than asking for help or admitting when we are wrong. But how do we get over these insecurities? How do we avoid getting defensive? The first step, in my opinion, is to recognize when you're behaving abnormally and relax. Stop taking everything so seriously and breathe. The world is not ending, you're not getting fired, and people will still respect you. Actually, if you admit when you're wrong and you ask for help, people will respect you more!

Allow me here also to use this space as an opportunity to point out that as a white, heterosexual male, I, societally, have more privilege in this area to push against the norms. Many people in underrepresented populations, such as women, disabled individuals, members of the LGBT community, or even those with really thick accents are unfortunately stereotyped more quickly as being less qualified professionals. So to fight the uphill battle they face, those individuals must put extra effort into conforming to get the positions they deserve. I cannot begin to tell you how racist, classist, sexist, ableist, homophobic, and biased that is. We need to be better. By being stuck in our ways and keeping the tradition of professionalism alive, we are also holding back many highly skilled and eager people, and that is simply not right.

Remember, one of the key roles of authentic leaders is to empower others to be their best authentic selves. Think about a time when you were at your best. Think about one of your happiest memories. What emotions were you experiencing? What allowed you to be so present in the situation? Were you trying to impress anyone? What were you thinking about?

DO YOU TAKE YOURSELF TOO SERIOUSLY?

Look at the people around you. How can you help others create those emotions? You can do it by giving them permission to be themselves. But they won't open up if you don't show them it is safe to do so. Think about your organization's values. What do you want your organization's members to say about how you made them feel? It is up to you to mirror your expectations of others. We have all heard the phrase, "Work hard, play hard." It's my firm belief that work and play do not have to be mutually exclusive.

Remember, as my friend Chris said, "You do not have to take yourself seriously to take your job seriously." In my opinion, that means: Allow yourself to be you at work. Laugh more, have a sense of play, let others in, and form respect-based relationships. Do all of that while doing what you need to get done to the best of your ability. Then you will feel more authentic and rewarded at work.

CHAPTER 10
DOES YOUR TITLE DEFINE YOU?

*As leaders, it is not only your job to impact others' lives,
but to let them impact yours.*

Earlier today, I was sitting in the Lincoln Street Diner in Ithaca, New York, enjoying some chicken and biscuits. Ithaca is home to both Ithaca College and Cornell University. As I am prone to do, I struck up a conversation with the manager about the area. An elderly woman, a couple of stools down, joined in the fun upon finishing her meal. As she was leaving, she told me, "You have to be careful what you say around here—you never know when you're sitting next to a Nobel Prize winner." I politely agreed with her as she paid her bill and left. I think I agreed to placate her in the moment, but I had not yet processed what she had said. As I sat down later to write, I thought more deeply about it.

If I knew the person I was speaking to was a Nobel Prize winner, would I interact with her differently? Would I be extra-respectful? Would I speak with a tone of admiration? Would I play off my awe by being delightfully sarcastic? Or would I just talk to that person as a fellow human being—as I would talk to anyone else?

What if I didn't know the person was a Nobel Prize winner at first, but the accolade came up later in our conversation? Would I change my manner of speaking mid-stream? Would I immediately feel insecure and fumble my words? Or would nothing change? Ultimately, should I change how I am acting because the person has the title of Nobel Prize winner?

Titles and labels play a large role in many aspects of our lives, both in professional and personal settings. They can be positive, but they can also be detrimental to our authenticity as leaders. Many of us are a bit title-obsessed. Title awareness happens in one of two ways: 1) Person A *asks* Person B what her title is, or 2) Person B *tells* Person A her title. Let's break both of these scenarios down because they have very different implications.

Instances of the first scenario are easy to find. For example, whenever we find out so-and-so went on a date with so-and-so, we immediately ask things like, "Are you a couple? Are you official? Are you hooking-up? Are you exclusive? Did you put it on Facebook?" Like it's any of our business! But we ask because: A) We are nosy, and B) We need to know what to label it so we can file it in our brain in a compartment that makes sense to us. It happens in our organizations as well. When you are meeting people around a new workplace, it's commonplace to ask people what they do or what their titles are. We always like to know everyone's title around us so we know where we fit into the bigger picture.

Wanting to find out how to refer to someone properly is natural. Most of the time, I feel we want to know this out of respect, for information, or out of innocent curiosity. It's part of our culture that would be hard to get away from. It's a value we place on one another routinely.

DOES YOUR TITLE DEFINE YOU?

The second scenario, where Person B *tells* Person A her title, is much more concerning in situations where sharing your title isn't really necessary, like it would be if you were conducting a job interview with a potential employee. When people tell me their titles the moment they introduce themselves to me in a social setting, I assume the sharer is either arrogant or insecure. Arrogance at the front end of a conversation is a surefire way to get me to do two things: 1) assume you are only interested in talking and not listening, and, as a result, 2) tune you out.

If you have done something incredibly impressive in your life, that is awesome. Your conversation partner will definitely listen to you and appreciate getting to hear your story from the source. However, if you do not ask the person at any point in the conversation about herself, the person will assume you do not care about her story. This does not mean that every conversation we engage in ultimately needs to be mutually beneficial, *but* people want to engage with you and your story, not just hear you recite your resume, biography, IMDB, or Wikipedia page.

Having a title doesn't mean you get to brag about it to others. Authentic leaders are not defined by their successes; they are defined by their abilities to share their stories and wisdom *while* admitting they don't have all of the answers. Having a title means you've earned a responsibility to share your knowledge with others.

> If you have knowledge and you're not sharing it,
> you're wasting everyone else's time.

We should be excited to share what we have learned. People who live their lives through their titles are missing the point. If we let our titles define us and don't own the fact that we do not have all the answers, we close ourselves off to the world. By letting a title or accolade define us, we settle on a plateau rather than striving to reach the mountaintop.

One of the greatest men I have met in my life is Vincent DeCola. He and I worked closely together at a university in New York. Vin communicated with students by first forming relationships with them. He would meet them where they were at and then mentor them from that point. He would talk with them about whatever they wanted—relationships, theater, the city, etc. He dedicated hours to getting to know each student on a personal level; the amount of time he invested in each individual was very impressive. Though it was not in his job description to do so, Vin would come to every single one of my residence hall staff meetings, which sometimes ran until 10:00 p.m. He was also sure to be an active participant in all of our staff activities. He was unquestionably working in higher education for the right reasons.

Vin spent time with me, too. We would go out to lunch and talk all about Gilbert and Sullivan productions, our families, and comedy. I would ask him a lot about his experience before working in his current job and about his travels. He would always ask me about my philosophy of working with student leaders and where I felt the university could improve its support for students. We had a wonderful friendship and were proud to call each other colleagues.

Here's the thing about Vin, though; he is maybe twenty to thirty years older than me, but that did not matter at all. He had previously been in charge of three middle schools, lived and worked in Micronesia for a while, and he helped run a volunteer corps that sent high school and college-age students to do volunteer work where it was needed most around the globe. Oh, wait, he is a Jesuit Priest, too.

I described Vin in the order I did because that is how it feels to get to know him. He first pours himself into being curious about you. As you get to know him, he will humbly tell you about his global knowledge and experiences. Also, he just happens to be a priest. If he led with the fact that he was a priest, it would immediately cause a conscious or subconscious reaction from the listener, so everything else Vin said or asked would be filtered through that biased (good, bad, or indifferent) lens. By not leading with his title, Vin allows people to get to know him as a person first. He is the person he is because of the work he has done, the people he has met, and life lessons he has learned...not because he is a priest. Not because of his title.

Vin is a perfect example of someone who is not done learning. He is a man who has had a ton of life experiences, but who still puts an emphasis on asking people, like me, lots of questions. Vin is forever curious about others, what their experiences are, and why they choose to lead others the way they do. He still wants to grow. He still wants to learn, and he knows that, in order to do so, he needs to engage others.

While writing this book, I have been reading blog posts, attending workshops, speaking with mentors, and then revisiting chapters I thought were done, only to rework them because others reshaped my thoughts. As an author, it is my hope to impact you, but I will also be re-shaped by the dialogue and feedback that this book creates after it is published.

So, to return to how I would react to speaking with a Nobel Prize winner, I guess my answer to that question would depend on how the other person carried herself. Is he or she arrogant? Humble? Proud? Excited? Nonchalant? Did she let the title of Nobel Prize winner define her, or was that just a gold star in her lifelong pursuit of learning? If it's the former, then to that I would say: the moment we let our titles get in the way of our learning is the exact moment we begin to fail. If it's the latter, then thank you for sharing your wisdom and passion with the world and asking me about mine.

No matter what title you have earned or been given, your work is not done. There is more to learn, to see, to do, and to accomplish. Congratulations on what you have done up to this point. You're allowed to celebrate your new job, latest achievement, and getting that starring role. That's awesome that you're in a new relationship and you got a raise. Enjoy that moment. Treat yourself to a vacation or a new toy, but then get back to learning. Everything you do and every person you meet has the ability to impact your life. But that only happens when you are open to it, when you realize the race of life is not over and you could be better.

If you let titles and labels define you, then you close the door on growth.

If I were to introduce you to someone, how should I do it? Are you a Mr.? Mrs.? Dr.? Ma'am? Ms.? Dean? President? Coach? Brother? Sister? Homie? Buddy? Chief? Mom? Dad? Are you so-and-so's partner? Should I say your full name? Your position at work? Your nickname? Your full name? Should I introduce you as My LGB or T friend? My mentor? My white friend? My coworker? An XYZ accolade achiever?

DOES YOUR TITLE DEFINE YOU?

Next time someone introduces you, ask her to leave out your title and not to label you. Let yourself be seen, first, as a human being. Start on a level playing field with the relationship—let it be mutually beneficial. It will give both of you the most opportunity to relate, find your common ground, bond, and then learn how the other person can positively impact you. It is my belief that as leaders, it is not only our job to impact others' lives, but to let them impact ours.

CHAPTER II
HOW DO YOU GET PEOPLE TO LISTEN?

Get them to listen; then get them to love.

As an authentic leadership speaker and personal coach, I have a pretty awesome day job. I like it so much that I often don't call it a job, and I rarely know what day of the week it is because all my days blend together. I get to travel around the world and share my experience-backed opinions, beliefs, and values with thousands every year, and most of those people actually listen! Many people I speak with ask me follow-up questions, want my business card, quote me on Twitter, follow me on Instagram, and share my blog posts. It is crazy and very flattering!

And you, you're reading my book! A collection of thoughts that I have compiled based on what I believe to be true at this point in my life. I am so unbelievably fortunate to have the opportunity to be on such a platform, so thank you. That said, I also recognize the responsibility I now carry with me. I am responsible for living my words. I must be a testament to my authentic leadership doctrine.

Throughout my journey of becoming a professional speaker, and just by being a fellow human being, I have learned the power of words. Ninety-five percent of the people I speak to every year have never heard of me. I am just some random guy who has a message that someone in a decision-making position thought would be beneficial for those people to hear. Or, more likely, my devastatingly attractive, fresh-dressing self rendered the decision-makers helpless so they had to book me. Either way, to my average audience member, I am just another speaker. I get introduced like any other speaker. I walk on stage like any other speaker. But then, I take the microphone and I am not like any other speaker.

There are two simple steps to give your message the best chance to be absorbed and effectively processed by your team or audience. First, get people to listen. Second, get them to love. Let's break those down.

I. Get them to listen.

Being a leader, much like being a public speaker, first means that you have to be good at relationship building. In a matter of moments, at the beginning of any interaction, you can go from being a stranger to anything you want, from oblivious to wise, humble to arrogant, or boring to engaging. As a speaker, it is my goal to be seen as authentic, educational, and entertaining...in that order. I know that if my message is going to stick, I must be seen as real to my audiences. The more the audience members can see themselves in me and in my stories, the longer I will have their attention. This point holds true for how you build rapport with your teams, as well.

HOW DO YOU GET PEOPLE TO LISTEN?

One of my biggest pet peeves when I listen to another speaker is a long introduction cataloging the speaker's successes and employment history. If you've read my chapters in order, this pet peeve shouldn't shock you. When I hear a lengthy intro focused on a speaker's accolades, it does two things for me as an audience member: 1) It bores me...usually causing me to take out my cell phone, and 2) It can make me feel insecure about my own accomplishments...meaning it can make the speaker unrelatable and her call to action feel unreachable to me. Neither of those things is a desirable jumping-off point for relationship building.

If I have heard of you, congratulations! I am ready to hear you speak. If I haven't heard of you, congratulations! I am ready to hear you speak. No matter what you have done with your life, if you have the ability to tell your story in a relatable and authentic manner, you will have my attention. Credentialing yourself, or having someone do it for you at your introduction, will only be moderately impressive for the first five minutes of your talk if you're then going to talk down to me for the next fifty-five minutes through a condescending delivery. And for those other fifty-five minutes, I will be thinking about what kind of burger I'm going to get after your talk and how many times my latest witty gem on Twitter will get re-tweeted.

This situation also holds true when you are in a position of influence. Congratulations that you have a title; you probably have more experience than those you are responsible for, and you have "been there and done that." If I report to you, however, then your reminding me of that title and experience feels like a display of power, not a vote of confidence. Connect with me, build me up, and bring me with you—

do not tell me you're awesome because it reminds me that I am not, and you can't then expect me to feel empowered to work with you.

Another inauthentic speaker pet peeve of mine is when a speaker makes the obvious effort to sound profound. I like cheese just as much as the next guy, but if all you're feeding me throughout your whole speech are cheesy lines with no substance in between, I am going to call you out. As a speaker, it is one of my jobs to meet the audience members where they are. I must respect and acknowledge their intelligence while challenging them to expand their views. I must also recognize the limitations of my own experience and knowledge base. That allows me to grow when challenged, rather than recoiling and getting defensive.

Just as it is my job as a speaker to meet my listeners where they are, so it's your job as a leader to do the same with your team members. Hanging twelve motivational cat posters around the office, though adorable, is not enough. Sending out a quote of the day is great, but make it the catalyst for a bigger dialogue. Setting expectations for work quality is smart—give people something to strive for, but....

We can't place expectations on others that we know we cannot live up to.

The strongest relationships I have were built on a foundation of listening and acceptance. That holds true for my relationship with my audiences. As ironic as it may seem, speakers must listen. We listen before speeches to the event planners, who will paint a picture of whom we are about to encounter. We also listen during our speeches. The people in the audience tell you exactly how you are doing; if you listen and read their body language, they tell you whether they are engaged, bored, over it, aggravated, happy, etc. We also listen after speeches to feedback about what worked and what did not. Speakers who ignore these cues miss opportunities to establish relationships.

How do you show your team members you are listening to them?

Having vision and an end goal in mind is crucial for any successful venture. However, being 100 percent steadfast in believing that your way is the only way to reach your goal will ruin so many partnerships; yes, you may accomplish what you want, but no one will be there to celebrate it with you. My dad consistently reminds me never to burn bridges. There is almost always a way that you as a leader can say, "No," while still making your team feel validated. Take the time, make sure the people around you feel heard, and always stay flexible.

Just like leaders, speakers must be flexible; they must be ready to manipulate their talks to reconnect with their audiences when needed. If you are going to ask your people for their ears, you must give them yours, too.

One specific time when I had to be flexible occurred when I spoke at a university in Arizona. The speech had been scheduled months in advance. When I landed after my flight from New York, I had a voice-mail from the event planner saying that one of the student leaders had been tragically killed the day before so they were trying to figure out how they wanted to handle it. The needless loss of this student's life was having an immense impact on the campus community. I felt and still feel awful for all of those who were affected.

I called my contact and said whatever they decided to do I would completely understand, and I would be there to help however they saw fit, if at all. She then informed me that the night before, the students had rallied together and held a candlelight vigil for their friend. Also, in a recent meeting with the planning committee, they had decided to move forward with my talk that evening because they thought some laughter would be good for the healing process.

Fast forward to that evening. About twenty minutes before I was supposed to go on, the event planner told me that before I spoke, they were going to have the victim's best friend and fraternity brother say a few words about the tragedy; then they would introduce me.

Side note: For those of you who have not heard me speak, the first five to eight minutes of my talk are high energy and basically straight out of my stand-up comedy routine with some crowd work. I begin this way because humor punches insecurity in the face. Therefore, it is a great way to knock down the walls people put up whenever they meet someone for the first time; it allows the relationship-building process to begin.

Needless to say, after the victim's fraternity brother and best friend spoke about him, there was not a dry eye in the house, including mine. He attempted to lighten the mood or at least provide some transition by saying how important it was for us to laugh because his friend had been on the school's improv team and would have done anything to make others smile. Then he introduced me.

For a high-energy speaker whose talks are infused with comedy and hard-hitting points, I needed to recognize how small I was in the grand scheme of things before taking the stage. I knew I could not go right from that beautiful and heart-wrenching moment into high-fives, giggles, and leadership development. So I took the first five to ten minutes of my speech just to talk to my audience about the tragedy. I spoke to the students and faculty about the gravity of what they were going through, and I applauded them for their ability to mobilize quickly and come together as a community for the candlelight vigil. I briefly shared my experiences with losing loved ones, and I encouraged them to keep sharing memories with each other. I then called out the awkwardness of having to transition from that moment into a light-hearted talk about empowerment. Before jumping into my talk, I asked for their permission to transition, welcomed them to laugh with me during my talk, and told them to feel free to come process anything and everything with me after. During my talk, I took mental notes on where the audience members were; fortunately, I think the majority of them were at a place where the escape from the weight was welcomed. But I know that the only reason my message was heard that evening was because I listened to the audience at the start.

The moment anyone speaking to an audience thinks he is bigger than that audience is the moment the speaker loses his listeners. Your friend and mine, Spiderman, once said, "With great power comes great responsibility." Anyone with a microphone in front of an audience has the power of influence. That power cannot be taken for granted or abused by a speaker. It must be respected.

2. Get them to love.

Once people in the audience see a speaker is authentic, they let their guards down and are more willing to accept the speaker's thoughts as wisdom. When we let our guards down, we allow ourselves to let more powerful emotions in, such as love. I aim for my talks to feel more like conversations than lectures. That relaxed atmosphere is trust-inducing. After that space is created, a speaker's points can be heard, processed, and applied.

If speakers instead come from a place of, "Dear audience, you're welcome I am here; look at all I've done, so feel free to bask in my glory," they would have their listeners' ears for a little while, but they will never have the audience's trust. If a speaker does not have the audience's trust, then her points will almost certainly be ignored or taken less seriously.

These same ideals ring true for you and anyone who has influence over others, whether it is in the boardroom, the classroom, a student organization, your family, your congregation, etc. I have seen speakers, CEOs, student organization presidents, and parents all fall into the "You're welcome" mindset I mentioned above. Their listeners immediately turn off and hear something more like Charlie Brown's mom than the message being delivered. Just because you have power in your position does not mean you have control. Trust-built relationships are still at the core of any movement or teambuilding.

My point is that we must first come from a place of, "Hello, fellow human beings," versus a place of, "Hello, subordinates." It's important to remember that we all are educators, and the best teachers we have ever had all first met us where we were. They assessed the talent/knowledge in the room, and then they jumped into teaching rather than starting above our heads and expecting us to "catch up." It is easier to push people to success than it is to pull them, and the learner will get more out of the pushing process. Remember, leaders push; they don't pull.

I had a Spanish teacher once who was a perfect example of how pulling does not work. The first day of class, she came into the classroom and immediately started speaking to us in Español. The students looked around at each other and laughed nervously at first, but then the laughter turned into fear. The teacher asked a couple of people questions in Spanish and got crickets as a response. After that happened a few times, she berated the class, saying things like, "You all know you're in a Spanish class, right?" Now I love and played team sports as much as the next student, but I didn't realize I had signed up with the, tough as nails, "Vince Lombardi" of foreign language teachers.

Sure, everyone in the class had taken a Spanish class or two before, but after a summer of caddying in the Hamptons, staying up to obscene hours with friends, and frolicking in sprinklers, my brain was not exactly ready for all that. That does not mean that I needed to be babied the first few days of class. Getting slapped back to reality is not always a bad thing, but this teacher turned the whole class against her on the first day! In that moment, she missed a crucial rapport-building opportunity. That's exactly what happens when leaders do not take a few moments to assess where their team is and get the team members onto their sides.

Get people to listen; then get them to love. We must approach leading as if we are building a relationship. Don't assume too much, don't spend an inordinate amount of time credentialing yourself, and don't just jump right in to your point. Instead, assess your team members, listen to see whether they are with you, and make sure they know you are a fellow human being. First, get their ears: put them on your side by authentically relating to them. Then they will trust you on the journey you want to take them on, and they will be willing to grow with you: you will have their hearts.

CHAPTER 12
DO YOU SPEAK IN LONG DIVISION?

Personal connections make tough conversations heartfelt instead of hard.

Was anyone else like me when it came to elementary and middle school math? I would take addition and multiplication over subtraction and division any day. I don't really know why; maybe they were easier, or maybe it was the budding optimist screaming inside me! Either way, I especially could not stand long division. It took too long and took up too much paper, and sometimes, you didn't even wind up with an exact answer! Divide 2041 by 33 and you get 61.8484848... with a remainder of the frustration over the loss of my hopes and dreams and time I'll never get back.

The calculator is a beautiful invention, and one I wish we were allowed to use early in our learning of mathematics. Then we could push past the "how to do it" and get to the "real world application" of math that would have been more engaging and applicable later in life.

Note: I mean no disrespect to math teachers; mine played a valuable role in my education. I'm just saying we are not going back to abacuses and slide-rules any time soon. If I were a math teacher, I think I would have more fun focusing on the application piece of what I'm teaching. Maybe I'm alone on that; maybe I'm going to get beat up by a bunch of math teachers, each of whom will leave 5! bruises on me. (5! = 120 for those playing at home who forgot their factorials) Either way, technology helps us be more efficient in our lives and, hopefully, it allows us to spend more time doing the things we love vs. completing menial tasks.

As much as I love technology, though, there is at least one area where we cannot rely on it: interpersonal concerns. In fact, interpersonal problems in our organizations will never be effectively fixed by texting or emailing. These are passive forms of communication. If members are slacking off, chronically showing up late for meetings, not paying dues, making inappropriate decisions that should be made above them, etc., a text message or guilt-trippy email is unlikely to cause them suddenly to change course. The technique we must employ is the long-division equivalent to text messaging: a face-to-face conversation.

Talking face-to-face is hard. When you have to give difficult feedback, it's awkward. It's time-consuming. But it's effective. Remember that nice text you got one time thanking you for doing something? Yeah, me neither. Remember that time someone asked you to go out for coffee or tea just to tell you how what you did made a positive impact on her? Heck yeah, I do! The same thing works for developmental moments that leaders need to have with their members. Texts can be deleted or dismissed with an Emoji reply. Emails can be read and scoffed at, then left to die in the inbox abyss. Face-to-face conversations, on the other hand, are much harder to be ignored, and they also promote two-way communication; having one tells the other person that you are open to hearing what she has to say, too.

All humans value time. We know how precious it is and how we would love to have more of it. We wish weekends and vacations were longer and that meetings would be more efficient so we had more time to complete the tasks we assign ourselves in meetings. The fact of the matter is that most of us are members of "Tired and Busy International." It's one of the largest, fastest-growing organizations in the world, but it lacks leadership because no one prioritizes it. Ask the person next to you, "How are you?" or "How have you been?" My money says they are in the organization as well.

Besides our own time, we usually try to respect others' time as well.

> That's why, when people go out of their way to sit down with us to have face-to-face conversations, it carries more weight.

This holds true for both positive and negative conversations.

As a supervisor, if I noticed that one of my supervisees was starting to slip in her duties, I would ask her to go for a walk or come grab a coffee. There is something very different about having a conversation outside of the workplace compared to having one in your office. It's like we all still have this fear of being sent to the principal's office from elementary school. When you are called into your boss' office, you have to go sit in front of the executive assistant, who not only doesn't bother getting out of his chair to greet you, but who casts knowing, condescending glares at you until your boss finally calls you in. It's an unnerving feeling and you walk in either defensive or scared right off the bat! I always try to avoid sparking that emotion in my supervisees by having tough conversations on more even playing fields.

Next time you have a team member not fulfilling her responsibilities or working against your organization's mission, invite the person out of the office to go for a walk or ice cream. Get out of the office or off campus and share what you have noticed, why it's a concern, and what you hope to change. If that's not possible, at least meet in a conference room on a different floor. The first step to having a healthy conversation—equal playing ground.

The next step is to listen. Everyone around you wants to be valued and treated as a fellow human being. When we send reprimanding directives via email, it takes a lot of power away from the person we are sending it to. It also often creates the image that the person's emotions are not important to us. Empathy is a critical skill for leaders to have.

The members of our organization have lives outside of work; they have relationships and responsibilities that exist beyond the walls of work. They have mothers in failing health, children who need to be shuttled around to practices, spouses who had bad days and need to talk, gardens that need to be weeded, and their own personal health to think about, too. If we act as though this is not the case and make assumptions about why people are slipping on their responsibilities, then we mistakenly take others' humanity out of the equation.

That's why whenever I have face-to-face conversations with people who have dropped the ball, I first ask whether something bigger is going on in their lives. If something is going on, then it's important for me to know that so I can frame my expectations of them. If nothing big is going on and they have been repeatedly slacking off or making inappropriate choices, I then dive into the potentially awkward, but necessary, conversation about performance and expectations. I ask whether they are still passionate about the organization, and if not, I ask why are they still in it? If they no longer care, we talk about whether the position is a good fit, and whether they should continue or what we can do to reinvigorate them. If they do still care about the organization and their roles within it, then together we come up with a course of action to improve performance and help them find meaning in their work. If they don't, then it may be time to coach them out of their current roles.

We all know there is a difference between a good friend and a good coworker. I remember one gentleman I worked with who was a really cool and fun guy. We would go out to lunch and giggle like school girls over pizza. I loved hanging out with him outside of the office, but at work, all he would do was complain. He didn't like his boss, so he would frequently come sit in my office and just vent. I asked him repeatedly why he stayed in a position that left him unfulfilled. He would always reply with, "I know; I just need to start searching for something else." But he never would. In other interactions, I would try to get him to visualize himself in a job where he wasn't frustrated: "What would a job you loved look like? How would your work and personal life be different?" I went so far as to role-play conversations he could have with his boss about it all. After listening to his complaints for six months, my opinions about him changed. Sure, he was still fun outside of work, but his crankiness, coupled with a lack of action, caused me to question his integrity. I started tuning him out. Alas, he is still in that position five years later. I learned from this experience that you can't be there for someone who can't be there for himself.

We are all scared of having the "Maybe you should look for another opportunity" conversation with individuals with whom we have relationships. They can be gut-wrenching talks and can spark very defensive reactions. The very thing that makes it hyper-awkward, though, is the same thing that makes it easier—the relationship's authentic history. The more time you have invested in someone, the more you want the best for that person. Because you know what motivates her, you can help her see how her needs are not being met in her current position and help her explore other opportunities. If that is the angle from which you approach these conversations, then they will be easier.

Some supervisors also have an understandable fear of being taken advantage of. That happened to me early in my career. I walked the line between friend and supervisor very finely. I did this intentionally because I thought that line was where trust and loyalty were built – which I still believe to be true. It, unfortunately, backfired on me early in my career because I was not yet good at holding people accountable to the expectations I set in the beginning of the year, and my staff knew it. When this situation started to become detrimental, a number of my staff members did the right thing and talked to me about their frustrations. They said it felt like I was playing favorites because others were being rewarded for not doing everything they were supposed to. Sadly, that was true; a couple of people were always taking advantage of me. They half-assed their responsibilities, and I only slapped them on their wrists. My problem was that in the beginning, I was too concerned with my staff liking me. I thought if I reprimanded them for not doing what they were supposed to, it would ruin the family-like team I was trying to create. What I learned is if you do not do what you say you will, and if you do not hold people accountable to the expectations you set, then you will fall too far on the friend side of the supervisor/friend line.

It is extremely important to find the right balance as an authentic leader. When emotions are out of the equation, the world is unrealistically black and white. "You didn't do X? Well, then, you now have to do Y or you're out." In my mind, that kind of inflexibility will only cause fear and resentment among those on your team. It comes back to what kind of workplace environment you are trying to create for your colleagues. At the end of the day, deadlines have to be hit, projections must be met, and people need to do their jobs. But if we take out the human element and expect everyone to be emotionless laborers, then burnout will be just around the corner and people will have no sense of loyalty to their employers.

I have a friend, Mike, who worked for an engineering firm that did not care about its employees. This firm's idea of creating a better work/life balance for their employees was to give them each a laptop so they could do work at home. Mike and his wife were expecting their second child, but the company couldn't have cared less. Mike's days consisted of waking up early, dropping off his daughter at day-care, working for 9-10 hours in the office, hopefully being able to pick up his daughter from daycare (if not, his pregnant wife would have to), coming home to eat a quick dinner, getting his child bathed and ready for bed, and then around 8:30, jumping on his laptop to work until he fell asleep on it.

After Mike's son was born, the firm did not let him take the vacation days he had earned because it had a big proposal due and Mike was the best, so he had to do it. About a month later, Mike quit and has not looked back. He now works for a firm that realizes the happier he is at home, the more productive he'll be at work and the longer he'll be committed to the firm. His new firm is right. Now Mike can respect the time he gives to his work because his work respects the time he needs at home.

Walking the line between being a supervisor and being a friend is potentially a slippery slope. But I think it is a line worth walking because it reminds us and those around us that we all have lives outside of the office, and sometimes, it is hard to leave that life at home. I am not saying we all need to be drinking buddies and have cuddle-puddles at work, but trying to approach every situation at work as if it is black and white is unrealistic and unhelpful. The positive culture we should be trying to cultivate is done using empathy and support.

The time is now to start prioritizing having more face-to-face conversations with your team. It's a priority in good times and in bad. These longer conversations in lieu of emails or texts will be potentially difficult. But if you have done a good job establishing a rapport with your team members, then they will respect you for taking the time to sit down with them.

Practice empathetic listening while not forgetting to hold people accountable.

It is a tough balance, but the best leaders do it very well. We have to stop taking the easy way out, so we must avoid delivering critical feedback electronically. Take the time, be present, do it correctly, and then in the end, just like with long division, you'll get the right answer.

What's your supervision style? Who is someone you need to have a potentially difficult one-on-one conversation with? Where can you meet with that person outside of the office? Set a deadline for yourself to make it happen. Where do you draw the line between friend and supervisor? Who are some leaders you have worked with whom you felt handled both sides well? How did they do it?

CHAPTER 13
WHAT IS YOUR PURPOSE?

Your intent will influence your impact.

Have you ever worked with someone you know is in his current role only because it's a resume builder? Or because he just wanted the title? It's terrible. The individual does not follow through on anything he says he will, he is seemingly elsewhere in meetings, and when he does speak, his contributions are normally limited to off-topic, flippant remarks; he is clearly burnt-out after little to no effort. People like that lack purpose.

I remember going into my senior year of high school and really wanting to be the President of the National Honor Society. I had to give a speech to my peers about why I should be the president. As you can tell by reading this stupidly, good book, I have mastered the art of manipulating the English language into captivating prose for the benefit of humanity. So, needless to say, I killed the speech and became co-president with my friend, Amy.

To say I did nothing during my term as president would be an understatement. Thank goodness Amy had her stuff together; otherwise,

I may have had to do something. Looking back at that time, I can honestly say that I only ran for president for two reasons: 1) for my resume, and 2) because I thought it would be cool to say that I was "the president." Since these two things—and these two things exclusively—were my intent at the time (read: my purpose), immediately after achieving both of them, I masterfully checked out. I would show up to meetings late and forget deadlines. I frequently would show up to meetings and ask Amy what we were supposed to talk about. It was not a good look. I cannot wait to see Amy's reaction when she finds out I wrote a book on leadership because when we worked together, I effectively wasted everyone's time—including my own.

Our own sense of purpose is a constantly evolving beast. Before high school, you depend on others; in high school, you figure out who you are. In college, you figure out why you are who you are—your purpose. Then in your mid-twenties, you face a fork in the road—Option 1: I take any job I can get my hands on with a good salary and health benefits so I can be more comfortable in life, or Option #2: I follow my passion, my purpose, now and bust my ass so it works out.

People who choose Option #1 are often the individuals who wake up one day in their mid-forties and ask, "What happened? Where did my life go? I never pictured any of this." They are not necessarily unhappy, but they realize their lives are not fulfilling.

They sacrificed their purpose to be content.

This moment of realization commonly leads to a mid-life crisis. Crisis is a strong but potentially appropriate word if that moment is not intentionally reflected on. Otherwise, brash selfish decisions are made by people trying to regain ownership of their lives. You hear about people buying flashy cars, cheating on their partners, becoming bitter toward their families, etc. It doesn't have to be a crisis, though. As I said, if we take time to communicate our realization with ourselves and others we trust, we can take appropriate measures to add value to our lives and restore our sense of purpose in who we are.

People who take Option #2 and follow their passions right out of college, or shortly thereafter, often struggle for a while. They have friends who chose Option #1 and are now making more money than them; those friends are buying houses and starting families. Seeing that sometimes really weighs on Option #2 people. At times, they are taking unpaid internships, going back for more school, working a few jobs, living back at home with their parents, or living with eight random people in a "converted" three-bedroom apartment. Things like connections and/or wealthy parents can sometimes alleviate some of this situation, but they can't alleviate the mental strain it puts on individuals who are hungry to get noticed doing what they love.

It is important to realize that your purpose is deeper than you may think it is. For example, a child who saves up all of her money to buy a bike does not have the purpose of saving to buy a bike. It's what the bike represents that drives her. Perhaps the bike means freedom. It gives her the ability to go see her friends and not have to rely on her parents to take her. Maybe the wind in her hair is almost spiritual to her, and she uses her time on her bike to think. Perhaps it represents her ability to get away from the home she lives in because it's a negative environment and the bike represents an escape. We all have wants in our lives, but it is what acquiring the object of our desire *means* to us that drives us. In short, it's the "why," not the "what," that matters.

The same principle applies to our work environments. Most companies have a mission statement that espouses the values and purposes of what they do. As an employee, you drink the Kool-Aid, completely embody the mission, and make it your daily purpose to bring this vision to life, right? NO! The mission statement is the company's purpose, but your purpose within that company is likely quite different. In fact, successful companies hire employees of varying skill sets and celebrate those differences so each employee feels empowered to do what he or she does best and bring different facets of the company's mission statement to life. It is important as an employee to know and agree with the company's mission.

Only when the employee understands and believes in her own personal purpose within the mission does she feel fulfilled at work.

Most of the thoughts about finding your purpose in life boil down to a very true clichéd phrase: "Love what you do." If you don't love what you do, then never settle for it, but keep doing it long enough to come up with a realistic plan for how you can live doing something you love.

I feel like right after we tell people to do what they love, we need to follow it up with another phrase, "and love where you do it." Few things are more frustrating than having a job you love while hating the people and/or the environment where you work. I have had the opportunity to be on both sides of this situation during my career.

WHAT IS YOUR PURPOSE?

Let's start with the bad. A place where I loved what I did but greatly disliked where I did it was at a prestigious university in New York City. My job as a resident director was to oversee the development of a successful community of first-year students in the residence halls on campus. I hired, trained, and supervised a staff of resident student leaders, advised a couple of student organizations, and helped create a safe community for our students to call home. The students I got to work with were just awesome. They were eager to connect, laugh, and learn. Not a bad deal if you ask me!

The issue was that the people in the upper administration and I had very different views on the purpose of the work we did. They thought the purpose was to run a business, make money, and crank students out with degrees. I thought the purpose was to help students develop as leaders, get involved in their communities, and feel safe in their new "home." Don't get me wrong; if you read the mission statement of the university, you would be impressed. I know I believed in it. It was upper administration's accolade-centric approach that was incongruent with the mission. We would survey students every year to make sure we were satisfying that mission, but when the students pointed out where we were failing, no changes would be made and the results were never published. The college experience of the current students (who were paying over $50K per year) was being sacrificed to try to gain a point or two in the next year's rankings. Students had minimal say in anything, and there was no such thing as advising or supervising—student development was pretty far down on the university's priorities list. Everything was micromanaged with the fear of anyone outside the university seeing the school as anything less than perfect being the motivator for anyone to do anything.

I could go on, but I think you get the point—I loved what I did, but I hated where I did it. So I started job searching and gave myself a goal date to be out. Sadly, after a year and a half of searching and almost getting four or five jobs, I was not hired anywhere else, so I just quit on my goal date. My values had been compromised for long enough, and I did not want to grow bitter toward a field I loved so much.

Naturally, I then moved to Harlem and took a job as a paid free-style rapper for a tour bus experience company in Times Square. No really, that's 100 percent true, and it was awesome. Then after doing that for five months, I was hired by a university where I loved what I did *and* loved where I did it—New Jersey City University (NJCU).

As the student government advisor at New Jersey City University, it was my job to do leadership development with almost all of the student leaders on campus. I was able to help in the planning of new student orientation, student leadership retreats, and serve on various community service projects. On top of that, the people I worked with were amazing. In every profession, there is a group of people who "just get it"; they understand why they do what they do, and they live their purpose (talk the talk *and* walk the walk). At my previous school, only a few people were like that, and we would huddle together for warmth. At NJCU, my coworkers, with few exceptions, "just got it." The work we did was valued, and the students knew they were a part of something special. The vice president of student affairs, Dr. John Melendez, quickly became one of my role models by the way he was able to spend quality time with and relate to students, yet still hold his own in university politics. It was a truly inspiring place to work, and of course, it came with its quirks, but I felt validated that I was competent and my passion was renewed for the work I do in Student Affairs.

My purpose at both schools was relatively the same—oversee leadership development with student leaders while cultivating a safe space for them to mess up, learn, and succeed. The difference in upper-administration support and philosophies is what changed my level of self-confidence and, in turn, my level of happiness.

As a leader, it will be important to revisit your purpose in everything you do at various points every year. Neither the first institution I spoke about nor NJCU was perfect. It was during the frustrating times that I had to dig back down to my intent in taking those jobs. We are quick to get burnt out and make rash decisions if we do not pause and rethink why we are doing what we are doing. For example, it's easy to half-ass the construction of a piece of furniture you buy from Ikea because you get fed up with all of the instructions, but then you have to live with the crooked, less-stable entertainment center that *might* hold your new 60" TV. Whereas if you just take a break in the middle of putting it together, take a few breaths, and remind yourself why it's important to get it right, you'll jump back in with a revitalized sense of purpose and get it done right.

During those moments of frustration in your job, just pause. Leave the office for a little while and go buy a doughnut. While you're out, first call a loved one to vent, and then call your mentor in the field and talk to her about where your head is, what you're dealing with, and ask whether she has ever been frustrated doing something similar. Then call me and say, "Thank you."

A FINAL NOTE

Phew! We made it to the end! Grab yourself a drink and buy yourself a medal at the dollar store. Seriously, I cannot thank you enough for taking time to read my thoughts and stories about the importance of being authentic in leading others. I hope you have found this book to be introspective, validating, and motivational. I also hope you giggled a few times! Now, despite the end being in sight, there is work you need to do and changes that need to be made. What actions will you take?

Let this book serve as a pivot point for you to become a more authentic leader. Find strength in your own story and share it with those you think could benefit. We all have the capacity to educate. I challenge you to take action. Own who you are so you can be real to others.

By reading this book, you have either learned or been reminded of the price of trying to come off as perfect in your organization. Hopefully, you now understand the role that love must play in leadership. Recognize what it means truly to own who you are. Become conscious of how your morals must play a role in your decision-making process as a leader. Appreciate the difference between being a role model and being a hero. Grasp how to be a better public speaker by being more real to your audiences. Most importantly, you should now realize that *your story is good enough.*

On the lines below, write the ten things you are going to do to be a more authentic leader. How will you get out of your own way? Where will you find the courage to be vulnerable? What story will you share? When is the next time you can lead others through your imperfections? What can you do for yourself? Hire a life coach? Read another book? Watch all of Brené Brown's TED talks? Go out for ice cream with your mentor?

1. _____
2. _____
3. _____
4. _____
5. _____
6. _____
7. _____
8. _____
9. _____
10. _____

Now that you've read my book, I encourage you to contact me—send me an email (JamesTRobo@gmail.com), or reach out to me on social media (@JamesTRobo). Tell me what you liked and did not like about my book. I recognize that this is just the first edition of this book, so it will get better, tighter, and more meaningful with your feedback. Lastly, tell me how I can help you going forward. If you are inter-

A FINAL NOTE

ested, I would be thrilled to offer you a no-obligation, free coaching consultation via phone, Skype, or in person if you live nearby.

Thank you again for spending your time with me. Best of luck on your journey to becoming the best authentic leader you can be. I look forward to being imperfect with you.

ABOUT THE AUTHOR

James Robilotta is an author, professional speaker, personal coach, and entrepreneur. He speaks to willing and unwilling audiences internationally about authentic leadership and promoting memorability. As a speaker, he is doing the two things he loves the most: causing audiences to think critically about their leadership journeys and making people laugh! His thought-proving talks are infused with self-awareness and comedy stemming from his background as a trained stand-up and improv comedian.

James is also a personal coach. He loves helping people get out of their own ways to live the lives they deserve and be the leaders they are capable of becoming. His clients undergo purposeful life-changing and self-affirming transformations. His clientele ranges from CEOs to college students.

Originally from Sayville, New York, James attended the University of North Carolina, Wilmington as an undergrad. After studying marine biology, he then, *naturally*, pursued his masters in counseling, earning his degree in 2007 from Clemson University. James worked on college campuses for thirteen years, developing student leaders and higher education professionals before going full-time with his speaking and coaching career. He performs around the country with his freestyle rapping improv comedy team, North Coast (NorthCoastNYC. com). James now lives in New York with his beautiful wife, Jacqueline, and their two super-sweet puppies, Kyra and Sophie.

BOOK JAMES ROBILOTTA TO SPEAK AT YOUR NEXT EVENT

Looking for a charismatic speaker for your next conference, meeting, or retreat? James Robilotta is a world class speaker who talks internationally to over 14,000 people per year at corporate and college events. Each one of James' clients gets a speech specifically tailored to meet the organization's desired emotional response and learning outcomes.

James Robilotta effectively uses his background in stand-up and improv comedy to keep audiences engaged from beginning to end. Audiences members often say that James' talk was one of the most fun learning experiences they have had in a long time. A phenomenal storyteller, James uses his personal stories to wrap up audiences in his key points. His talks are laced with self-awareness, introspective moments, and an occasional pun.

Whether you are looking for a one-hour keynote to set the tone for your next conference or a three-hour workshop to dive deeper with your organization, James Robilotta is an excellent choice. James is not afraid to challenge attendees by going deeper, but he does so in a manner that makes people feel safe. Teams leave James' workshops more aware and close-knit than when they arrived.

Lastly, James Robilotta is also a phenomenal emcee. His contagious energy and quick wit keep audiences laughing and on their toes while he keeps your event on schedule!

For a free complimentary interview to decide whether
James is the right speaker for you, contact him at:
JamesTRobo@gmail.com or www.JamesTRobo.com

HIRE JAMES ROBILOTTA TO BE YOUR PERSONAL COACH

James Robilotta views his role as a coach as being similar to a new pair of glasses. It's his job to get you to define more clearly the vision you have for your life and the roadblocks you have put in the way of making it happen. A lot of the time we feel stuck in our everyday lives. It's the same routine every week: work, hang out with friends or family, watch TV, and sleep. Week, months, years go by, and then one day, our head pops off the pillow and we reflect on how our life is not at all where we thought it would be at our age. It's not too late to break the patterns and live the fulfilled life you deserve! Let's be honest; on the surface, Life Coaching sounds cheesy, but push past that. We all need someone to help us get out of our own way every once in awhile.

James' role as a coach is twofold: 1st) he will get you to shed light on the matters that are keeping you from actualizing your dreams, and 2nd) He is there to help hold you accountable for working toward your new, more freeing, lifestyle. After each session, James will challenge you to take steps toward reaching your goals and eliminating your self-doubt. Every time you reconnect, he will follow up and process your efforts, what worked, what didn't, and why. Often, our desire for greater fulfillment, money, and respect smacks up against our procrastination, hesitation, and resistance. Having someone hold you accountable will ensure you are always driving toward the life you deserve.

James is available for coaching in the following areas:

- Personal Coaching (getting un-stuck, relationships, moving toward your dreams, work/life balance)
- Leadership Coaching (leading authentically, communication styles, teamwork approaches, motivating yourself and others, supervision strategies)
- Public Speaking (overcoming fear, tips and tricks, content development, honest post-speech feedback)

It is time to own your insecurities, realize your passion, and regain control in your life. Contact James Robilotta to set up a FREE forty-five-minute conversation to learn about coaching, whether it is right for you, and if so, whether James would be your best choice for a coach!

JamesTRobo@gmail.com

www.JamesTRobo.com

CPSIA information can be obtained at www.ICGtesting.com
Printed in the USA
BVOW06*1351161015

422523BV00003B/6/P